The Prophet and Herland
A Comparative Analysis

Hoda Thabet, Ph.D

May 2016

The Prophet and Herland

Copyright © 2016 Hoda Thabet
Reykjavík 2016

National and University Library of Iceland ISBN: 978-9935-9256-1-9

Printed in Háskólaprent ehf. 2016

Table of Contents

Abstract

This paper investigates the influence of Herland by Charlotte Perkins Gilman (1860-1835) and The Prophet by Khalil Gibran (1883-1930) on American literature from the perspective of four major cultural institutions. In the literature currently available, there is little in reference to the influence of Gilman and Gibran- two marginalized writers at the beginning of the era of American realism- on the discourse of American literature.

The purpose of this study is to focus primarily on the works of Gibran examining how he depicts four vital cultural institutions. The researcher will compare another marginalized writer, Charlotte Perkins Gilman, with Gibran and both of their focuses on, and the impact of, four cultural institutions on their writing. The institutions focused on are family, education, religion, and love of country.

Gibran was a male who lived in an era when society oppressed women and considered them unequal to men. Gilman was a female who lived in the same era. Each has a very analytical, fictional approach to how things could be if they were different in real life. They are from two different traditions. Gibran was an Arab immigrant, who was a pioneer of Modern Arabic American literature. Gilman was an American woman living in a society where women are not valued nor considered equal to men. Many consider her a pioneer in feminism because of her in-depth look at women and their place in society in her writings.

There is value in analyzing the works of writers from two different traditions. The comparison and contrast between the two gives a basis for better understanding each. It further enhances the understanding of a literature work's impact on a historical era, as well as the impact that the historical era has on the literature of the time.

Doing a comparative study of literature from the same period and with similar themes leads to greater understanding of not only the literature but the society of the time. An examination of their literary comparisons between *Herland* and *The Prophet* and their impact on the culture of the era is a focus of this paper.

The structure of the intended analysis of *Herland* and *The Prophet* is as follows: to investigate three major factors. First, the researcher will examine Gibran's work in light of its place in the literature of its individual culture and in relation to transcendentalism. Second, the researcher will then examine Gilman's work in light of its culture. Finally, the researcher will compare the effect of *Herland* and *The Prophet* on four major cultural institutions of their era. The four investigated institutions included are family, religion, education, and love of country (patriotism).

Many scholars trace *Herland* and *The Prophet* in the study of American literature as pioneering iconic works. However, critical and cultural approaches proposed in the literary studies will compare the featured writings of Gibran to Gilman. The comparative study of inter-textual relation between *The Prophet* and *Herland* will define a more in-depth understanding of how their writing influenced the four institutions defining culture.

1 Introduction

This paper analyzes the literary significance of two marginalized writers in relation to American life and culture in the early twentieth century: Khalil Gibran (1883-1930), author of *The Prophet* (1923) and Charlotte Perkins Gilman (1860-1935), who wrote *Herland* (1915). They were contemporaries and spent portions of their early years in the neighboring states of Massachusetts and Connecticut, although neither knew the other. Each wrote fictional works as a way to explore how the lives of millions could be improved if opportunities for self-expression, spiritual development, educational attainment and pride in heritage were more widely fostered in American society. Both authors wrote to voice their moral vision; their idealism and disappointment with existing social institutions. In *The Prophet*, Gibran seeks to influence his readers to reject sectarian and nationalistic uses of religion and to embrace the unity of world religions and ethnicities. Gilman's *Herland* protests the limitations placed on intelligent and capable women and urges women to create institutions of their own in which to invent satisfying and creative lives.

The first part of this analysis will explore Gibran's writing of *The Prophet*, focusing on Gibran's place among the Arab-American writers of his era as well as on the impact of American transcendentalism on his world-view. Next comes a comparison of the ways that Gibran in *The Prophet* and Gilman in *Herland* used literature to critique four major cultural institutions: the family, religion, education, and national identity. This comparative study of *The Prophet* and *Herland* is undertaken to facilitate better understanding of how these literary works influenced American attitudes toward the four cultural institutions, if not immediately, then in the decades following the Depression and World War II.

It is hoped that a comparison of two authors who viewed life in the United States from the margins will deepen the reader's appreciation of the powerful attraction of democratic ideals to those least nourished by them. It concludes that each writer successfully critiques American social conservatism, Gibran in matters of ethnicity and religion and Gilman of gender. But neither steps beyond his or her received views on other matters; Gibran on conventional marriage and family roles and Gilman on Aryan racial and middle class strictures on sexual expression.

1.1 Examining two cultures

The purpose of this study is to focus on the works of two writers who address vital institutions in a culture and have a major impact on the development of American Literature. One was a male, Gibran, who lived in an era when society oppressed women and considered them unequal to men. The other was a female, Gilman, who lived in the same era. Each has a very analytical, fictional approach to how things could be if they were different in real life. They are from two different traditions. Gibran was an Arab immigrant, who was a pioneer of Modern Arabic literature. Gilman was an American woman living in a society where women are not valued nor considered equal to men. She is considered a pioneer in feminism because of her in-depth look at women and their place in society. She compared a matriarchal society and a patriarchal one (Kamal).

There is value in analyzing the works of writers from two different traditions. The comparison and contrast between the two gives a basis for better understanding each. They enhance the understanding of a literature work's impact on a historical era, as well as the impact that the historical era has on the literature of the time. An examination of their literary differences and their outlook on the culture of the era as impacted by their different traditions is a focus of this paper (Ganaie 5).

Doing a comparative study of literature involving similar forms and themes leads to further thought and the development of the understanding of new concepts. The comparison of the problems and subjects in different pieces of literature helps to give a connection between the literary works. It further leads to a fuller understanding of varying cultures, traditions, and histories (Ganaie 1). This study of the commonality of themes and problems addressed in the two pieces of literature further exposes the impact they had, collectively and individually, on American Literature of the time. Such a study further show the great impact these and other writers had on the political issues of the time in light of the impact their works had on the thinking and philosophy at the time.

Culture is defined by Maznevski as a pattern of differences in a society, especially those patterns involving deep values shared by a group of people (276). He further explains a number of elements to define how the institutions of a culture are assimilated (Maznevski et al. 276).

1.2 Literary focus of the time

To understand fully a literary work, or works, it is important not to look at just the societal, political, and cultural aspects of the era. One must also look at the literary focus. Several significant issues or focuses influenced the literature of the time. Some of these included: 1) mysticism, 2) feminism, 3) social inequality and immigration, and 4) financial extremism. An examination of each of these issues will enable one to make an informed look at their impact on the literature of the time.

The time during the writing of *Herland* (1915) and *The Prophet* (1923) were turbulent times with the beginning of the feminist movement, the racial unrest, and the focus on the growth of racial equality among the arts, socioeconomic extremes, sociopolitical unrest, and the beginning of a new focus on realism. This meant a greater potential for influence on the writings of the marginalized populations. Gibran was described as being "intensely aware of the social and political structure of their society and could identify the wrongs which were besetting the society" (Ganaie 111).

Gilman, likewise, was well aware of the social and political structure of society as it affected her views of a woman's status in that society. The consequence of this awareness resulted in Gilman challenging the very fiber of that society, the values defining family, home, religion, community, capitalism, and democracy as she witnessed them in her world (De Simone, D. 13).

Gilman proposed a completely new architecture for the woman's role in the home, a home that was different from what she currently considered normal. In her realistic fiction, she proposed four new models for the home. A cluster of realistic, fictional stories supported each suggested model of housing. These included:

1. Motels/boarding houses were the first group, used for the liberated, progressive women in the first cluster of stories.

2. The second group of stories depicted groups of residences connected by central facilities enabled the sharing of responsibilities for laundry, cooking, childcare, and cleaning.

3. The third suggestion was for alliances of women who met in clubhouses for networking and for receiving education for work outside the home.

4. The fourth cluster of stories depicted rehabilitative facilities, run by women for women.

Each cluster of stories depicted an architecture for women that was designed to encourage freedom from male dependency and personal growth or the woman (Allen   146).

1.3   Mysticism

The accepted description for mysticism is that it is a spiritual discipline. Practitioners of this discipline have had personal mystical experiences and have been and/or are in touch with a divine presence. They in turn strive to help society understand his mystical experience, because only a very few are aware of a divine presence and can visualize events outside the material. To enable these insights, the mystic must make use of intuition, instinct, visions, dreams and revelations, and special insights that are granted to him (Ganaie 78).

Mystics believe in a reality outside the everyday and physical. They believe one has to reach deeper than the material. It is believed that the communion is between an enlightened individual and God on an individual level (Ganaie 80).

1.3.1 Gibran as mystic

The name Sufism was given to Islamic mysticism. Though different descriptions were used, they all are parallel to an interior, esoteric relationship. It has its main aim to cleanse the spirit and bring the focus only on God. It enables one to be able to reach the Divine and purify the spiritual self. Islamic mysticism differs from Christian mysticism in that it has a continuous historically and has millions of followers (Ganaie 81).

Gibran is a mystic and prophet. He holds an apocalyptic vision of Man and God. He described the unity of existence by describing a coming together of disparate views. He opposed organized religion, but focused on an inner spiritual self, and had mysticism traits in his beliefs and work. He went beyond religion and culture into the mystic. He focused strongly on awakening, seeing, and perceiving, believing it was outside the common belief of individual perception. Gibran considered himself a spiritual messenger for heavenly beings (Ganaie 89).

Gibran was concerned with the tension between body and soul. He believed the soul defined a man. He strove to help people realize the divine. He believed firmly in imagination, believing God and man shared it. He believed man reaches perfection because God is in everything. He did believe that God is transcendental, but also believed that nature and the physical is the key to understanding the relationship between God and Self. He also believed in the harmony between one's body and soul, and that each one is somewhat of a prophet. He felt strongly the responsibility to guide people to see and understand their inner self (Ganaie 90).

Gibran used his talent as a writer to inform individuals of their dreams and visions. He had the uncanny talent to visualize the spiritual, which was considered by many to be above the normal (Ganaie 92).

1.3.2 Gilman as mystic

Gilman has been termed a poet, a preacher, an iconoclast, and a theoretician. She dealt in depth in her works, and in her personal life, with women's rights. As a theologian, she worked for the betterment of the human race (Allen 29).

Before her death, Gilman stated she was not interested in personal immorality. She said she was only interested in Humanity (capital H was hers) and that she was content with God (Allen 30). She believed she was a vital part of God, and that she was a vessel for divine energy. She drew strength from her personal mysticism more than anything else (Allen 35).

1.3.3 Feminism

Published in 1915, when women were beginning to question their roles as the "Other," and as objects of femininity, being expected to objectify her own self, *Herland* depicts a separatist feminist utopia (Cavataro 1). Gilman was able to write literature from her own experience that addressed the subject of the oppression of women (Baumgartner 5).

With *Herland*, Gilman first ventured into the realm of feminism, or the questioning of the relegated place of women by the male population and the entire society. Later works were even more concerned than this one, that merely looked at what she believed could be a Utopian society if women were given the proper significance (Kamal).

In *Broken Wings*, Gibran shows his perception of the place of women in society. It is from this perception that he writes about home and family. In this work, he indicates that a woman was considered a commodity, passed from one household to another (parents to husband). Gibran further says that women used to be happy to be a homemaker, but in modern civilization has become miserable. He said that woman used to walk blindly in light, but now walks with open eyes in the dark. Her beauty lay in her lack of knowledge and in simplicity, and strong in weakness. However, Gibran says, she now is ugly with knowledge that is superficial and heartless (Gibran, Broken Wings).

1.4 Social inequality

The Arab immigrants in the late nineteenth century and the early twentieth century found themselves not so welcomed in the Americas. They wished to endorse Americanization, but still to keep their Arab identity. The attitude toward immigrants complicated this. According to the definitions of who was qualified for naturalization, only "free white persons" were able to be naturalized, according to the Naturalization Act of 1790. The definition of "white" in the early 1900s excluded anyone with a darker skin tone, which included the Arabs. They fought for their rights to naturalization, but somewhat unsuccessfully. The treatment that the Arabs experienced set the precedence for the decision on whether or not to include an entire ethnic group (Majaj).

At the end of the nineteenth century, women had begun experiencing vocational and educational options that were previously unavailable to them. They realized they had options outside the common beliefs of the culture in that time. For the most part, women in this culture were confined to the option of vocation in the home, tending to their husbands and children (Lane 13).

Prior to the Civil War women were venturing into educational options, having access to several colleges by the time of the Civil War. After the War, several women's colleges were founded. This led to a new breed of women who demanded their place in the workforce and recognition for their accomplishments (Lane 14).

1.5   Financial extremism

The Arab immigrants came to America searching for their dreams. Instead, they found very difficult conditions and had to work hard to survive. They found hardship and disappointment instead of the dreams they hoped to fulfill in this new land. They were forced to sell goods throughout the streets, even though they did not know the language and tried to communicate by signs (Jafarovi & Ibrahimovaf 109).

In Gilman's world, society was a patriarchal one. Women were relegated to caring for children, husband, and the home. This placed women in a submissive position to men. Gilman thus attempted to redefine the role of women. She envisioned a well-educated person who was economically self-sufficient and politically active. These characteristics of women are seen in her writing of *Herland* (De Simone).

Because of their dependence on males for livelihood, women have been "denied the enlarged activities which have developed intelligence in man, denied the education of the will which only comes by freedom and power" (De Simone).To be truly free, De Simone believes, she must have access to higher education similar to that the males in their society. Only then can she enjoy freedom and economic independence.

1.6   Nineteenth century political influences

Two revolutions heavily influenced the nineteenth century, the French Revolution and the Industrial Revolution. This led to the loss of an old order based on relationships, property, class, religion, and monarchy. This meant there were huge changes in store. These included changes in population, conditions in labor, property, urbanization, technology, factory systems, and political masses. Though each of these is more or less a chance factor, because of the close relationship of literature to sociological conditions, each of these had an impact on the literature of the time of Gibran's and Gilman's writings.

One indicator of historical change is the development of new words or the revising in meaning of old ones. During the nineteenth, many new words and revisions were realized. Some of these were: industry, democracy, middle class, rationalism, collectivism, liberal/conservative, utilitarian, bureaucracy, and capitalism (Nisbet).

1.6.1   Population

During this period, population's numbers doubled. This negatively impacted the welfare of the people. It led to an overabundance of people dependent on a limited food supply, meaning many people suffered hunger. The poor, less educated class of people suffered this more than any other class. This resulted in a discrepancy in class standards, with a middle class coming into existence (Nisbet).

1.6.2   Conditions of labor

As society moved forward and industrialism got a firm grasp, large numbers of people moved out of traditional villages, parishes, and families and into industrial areas, resulting in slum areas. These slums were squalid and living conditions were atrocious. Wages were below cost of living, and families became larger, all contributing to a dismal economic outlook. Though in hindsight, recognition of these things were not as dismal as the seemed at the time, writers of the time still recognized the situation as dismal just the same. Their perception is more important than the actual situations (Nisbet).

1.6.3   Transformation of property

As the industrial era escalated, industry gradually took over property, with factories and workshops taking precedence. Additionally, they type of property changes as well. Instead of being land and money as in the past, it now included intangible property. Stock shares, negotiable equities, and bonds became more influential that "hard" property. This meant those with such property became dominant, meaning the distance between classes widened as money was realized by some through speculation. This allowed a few to enjoy this great wealth to be had, and their subsequent domination over others in the realm of lifestyle and politics (Nisbet).

1.6.4 Urbanization

Urbanization was the sudden movement of the population into towns and cities. In the past, cities were centers of freedom, culture, and the center of civilizations. Suddenly, they became centers of divided population groups, broken families, alienation, and the decline of values as people became anonymous. This led to a completely new concern about the problems of urbanization. This influenced not only literature, but also the social sciences (Nesbit).

1.6.5 Technology

The mechanization of this new era was widespread throughout factories and agriculture. This threatened to break the strong relationship of man and nature as had always been enjoyed. It even involved the distance between man and man, as well as distancing man from God. This led to the fear by thinkers and writers that humankind was going to become dehumanized. Many declared that the mind and spirit of humankind was being threatened, especially technology in industry. Opponents of technology objected on moral, psychological, and aesthetic grounds (Nesbit).

1.6.6 Factory systems

In addition to the problems with urbanization and mechanization, factory systems were established, which resulted in masses of persons working long hours in factories. These factories were the cause of extremely poor working conditions and low wages. They became a major concern of sociologists and writers, who attempted to institute reform (Nesbit).

1.7 Development of political masses

As changes took place in the nineteenth century, people began to become aware of their ability to change political situations by voting and participating in political processes. This led to the development of political masses. This contributed to political oppression for the disenfranchised population. Writers and thinkers were concerned about this political power of one class over another, and many attempted to increase awareness to give power to those who were being oppressed (Nisbet).

1.7.1   Twentieth century political influences

The twentieth century saw not only an extension of the nineteenth century developments, but also saw new developments of its own. The extent of these developments made those in the nineteenth century seem tame by comparison, giving an appearance of unity and without all the turbulence that the twentieth century saw.

The democratic and industrial revolutions, begun in the nineteenth century, grew with hindrance during the twentieth century, expanding throughout the societies in the west and moving to most all nations and localities. It moved also to non-Western areas as well. People who previously had lived in tribes, communities, pastoral settings, united in religion, suddenly found themselves under the influence of industrialism and a new technology (Nisbet).

Contrary to the common belief that solving issues of industrialization and organizations of society would take care of all problems in a society, it was just the opposite. Problems escalated once the basic needs of food and shelter. It appeared that as basic survival needs disappeared, humankind had a desire for fulfillment of other needs. There was a contrast of ideas, that of status, purpose, and community as opposed to alienation, lack of standards, and general breakdown of society. This shows the conflict in the nature of humankind (Nisbet).

1.7.2   Two World Wars

Two world wars in the same century took a great toll on life and property. These two wars alone had a greater toll than all previous wars in history combined.

1.7.3   Totalitarianism:
Communist, Fascist, and Nazi; and Terrorism

Terrorism, whether Communist, Fascist, or Nazi reached astronomical proportions and atrocities that was almost imaginable. Those who accepted science and technology, and who believed they were humane, were very devastated with what they observed (Nesbit).

1.7.4   Affluence

Though some people suffered in relationship to others in reference to working conditions and economic health, others enjoyed the benefits of an abundantly affluent society. Even those less affluent still enjoyed affluence previously unknown. The level of living continuously rose, with a resultant rise in expectations born of this affluence (Nesbit).

1.7.5   Social turbulence

The extreme turbulence of the twentieth century involved political, economic, and social desires. These had begun to escalate and filter to ethnic and racial minorities, eventually including whole continents. Each victory relating to freedom and rights just fueled the desire for what had not yet been realized (Nisbet).

2 Khalil Gibran: Life and Work

In order to understand an unconventional literary work, it is necessary to explore the social milieu in which it was written. Khalil Gibran, author of *The Prophet*, was born in Besharri, Lebanon, in the Lebanese Mountains, on January 6, 1883. His parents were Catholic Christians of the Maronite sect. Gibran was separated from the rich culture of his homeland at the age of twelve when he moved to America. In 1895, Gibran's mother took Gibran, his brother and their sisters with her, while her husband, a drinker and a gambler, was incarcerated (Cole).

In his early teens, Gibran attended Denison House, a school for poor children in South Boston, where he was encouraged to be an artist. He published a few of his drawings and posed for Boston photographer Fred Holland Day. His mother worked as a seamstress. In 1898, Gibran's mother returned him to Lebanon for further education. He lived there until 1903, returning to the USA upon the death of his sister, followed soon thereafter by the death of his mother and brother.

Upon his return to Boston, Gibran renewed his acquaintance with Fred Holland Day, who arranged an exhibition of Gibran's drawings in 1904. Day introduced Gibran to Elizabeth Haskell, a teacher ten years his senior who became a lifelong friend and sometime romantic partner. Supported by his surviving sister, Gibran studied art and traveled back and forth to Europe and Lebanon until 1910. After four years of Arabic studies in Beirut and a couple of years in Europe, Gibran returned to New York, where he lived until he died in 1931 (O'Connor 1-2). Despite two long lasting relationships with American women, Gibran never married, nor did he have children or become an American citizen. Gibran died at the age of 48 from tuberculosis and cirrhosis of the liver (Bushrui).

Many who study Khalil Gibran trace the cultural and literary influence of both East and West on his writing. Translator and editor Joseph Sheban observes that "Gibran's thirst had taken him to the fountains of Buddha, Zoroaster, Confucius, Voltaire, Rousseau, Nietzsche, Jefferson, Emerson, and even to Lincoln" (Sheban 54). Gibran became a mediator between the Arabic and the Western worlds, attempting to bridge the gap between them. He advocated a joining of his heritage and his new environment. He incorporated Western themes into his Arabic literature, while making his own contribution to the West.

Gibran published both in Arabic and English; a few of his books were published posthumously. These works include *Spirits Rebellious* (1908), *The Broken Wings* (1912), and *A Tear and a Smile* (1914), all written in Arabic; *The Procession* (1918), *The Madman* (1918), *The Forerunner* (1920), *The Prophet* (1923), *Sand and Foam* (1926), *Jesus, The Son of Man* (1928), *The Earth Gods* (1931), all in English; and the posthumous *The Wanderer* (1932), *The Garden of the Prophet* (1933), and *Lazarus and His Beloved* (1933).

2.1 Khalil Gibran as a Reformer of Arabic Literature

Khalil Gibran actively participated in the Arabic literary renaissance that began towards the end of the 19th century, along with individual writers in the Arab world, such as Butrus al-Bustami (1819-1883), Khalil Mutran (1872-1949), and Abbas Mahmud al-Aqqad (1889-1964). In the late nineteenth and early twentieth centuries, Arab writers began to come to America to escape the sociopolitical and economic hardships of their countries. They already had a strongly established literature from as early as the fifth century and brought with them valuable literary works. Their literature was borne of their views of real life, humanity, love, and the beauty of nature.

These Arab-American literates strove to reform the Arabic language as they attempted to integrate new ideas into traditional literature. Arab writers living in America – Mahjar writers – made an even more concentrated effort to change their conservative literature to be more attuned to Western poetry, including that of the English Romantics. Modern Arab-Americans adopted new styles that reflected the freedom they enjoyed, while they felt that their counterparts in the East, on the other hand, strove to maintain the status quo (Mcharek). They introduced the prose poem as well as Western individualism and secularism (Mcharek). A Mahjar writer, Mikhail Nuayma, was nominated for the Nobel Prize for Literature in 1964, proving that this rich heritage of literature influenced later world literature (Jafarov and Ibrahimovaf 201).

Gibran was a part of the Mahjar group of American immigrant writers who denounced Arab traditions that they thought had become stagnant, while attempting to revive Arabic literature in their new home. Gibran was also noticeably influenced by early Arabic writers, both intellectually and morally. These include such figures as Ibn Khaldun, Avicenna, Imam Ghazali, Abu Nuwas, and al-Mutanabbi (Günday). Indeed, the Arab Mahjar literature was born out of familiarity with classic Arab literature and melded with the experiences of adopted Western civilization and literature.

The depth of this new literature stemmed from homesickness, according to Jafarov and Ibrahimovaf (203). The Mahjar found themselves expected to adopt the dominant U. S. culture, a feat over which they agonized. The Arab immigrants came to America searching for their dreams. Instead, they found hardship and disappointment. They were forced to sell goods in the streets, even though they did not know English, so they tried to communicate by signs (Jafarovi and Ibrahimovaf 109). They did not know how to abide the pressures put on them to assimilate and yet to maintain their native identities. Their own newspapers and journals addressed these issues. The Mahjar writers discussed how to maintain their identity among members of the generation born in America as well as how best to best integrate into their adopted country (Majaj).

A further complication in their Americanization was the racism that the Arab immigrants experienced in the United States. The Immigration Act of 1917 excluded persons who were not white. The right of Arabs to become naturalized citizens of the USA was threatened because of their non-white status in the immigration office. It was left to the courts to decide whether an individual or an ethnic group qualified for naturalization. The Arabs were ruled not to qualify because they had darker skins and were not of European origin, whereas Syrians and Palestinians were classified as foreign-born whites.

Despite the difficulties they experienced, the Arab immigrants made gains in their socioeconomic status and literary achievements. Those who managed to learn the language obtained higher education and published their own periodicals in their language. The Mahjar writers wrote in both Arabic and English. Their writing, known as Mahjar or Arab-American writing, bridged the gap between East and West, combining the philosophical ideas of both, drawing upon the writings from "Al-Mutanabbi, Al-Farid, and al-Maari to Homer, Virgil, Milton, Emerson and Thoreau" (Majaj). Mahjar literature went through several developmental stages. Their works were valuable to American literature and definitely made an impact on it (Jafarov and Ibrahimovaf 200).

The works of these Mahjar writers spoke of homesickness, love, freedom and humanism. They broke away from traditional forms and themes and innovated with form and content to attract a wider audience. They sought to preserve their language and literature in the Americas, ensuring it met the demands of current literature but also introducing their innovative ideas and literary forms (Jafarov and Ibrahimovaf 201).

The Mahjar writers banded together to form special literary societies to help spread their influence as writers and to ensure the preservation of their literature. These societies developed over a number of years, each with a different focus, but with the purpose of spreading their writings throughout the "New World" in which they found themselves residing (Jafarov and Ibrahimovaf 195-

202). They fostered an ongoing debate about how to reconcile Christian and Islamic identity, Arab-American and white native born American citizens (Majaj).

Gibran was a pioneer among the Mahjar writers. Some of the Arab literary societies were formed during Gibran's time, and under his influence, including the very first, the Pen League, as well as the Minerva society, the Maari society, and the al-Adab society. Each of these made an impact for Mahjar literature, including promoting it, aiding new writers, and making it visible to the world in a positive manner. The different societies, each in its own way, helped to further the Mahjar literature. Whether short-lived or more lasting, they contributed in preserving and furthering the rich heritage of this proud people.

These writers were at odds with their social world that was corrupt, hypocritical, and materialistic (Ganaie 111). They strove to change the situation with their writings that focused on freedom, nature, real life, and love (Jafarov and Ibrahimovaf 200).

Mahjar literature had many characteristics typical for the Romantic style. In comparing Mahjar literature to the characteristics of Romanticism, it is evident that their literature more closely relates to Romanticism than Realism, though there was a transition from the first to the latter in the 19th and early twentieth centuries. One great difference from traditional Arabic literature was in Gibran's depiction of nature. In Arabic literature, nature was depicted as something to be contended with, while Gibran viewed it as having a life of its own. In *The Prophet* (21), he endowed it with spiritual, emotional, and intellectual properties: "Forget not that the earth delights to feel your bare feet and the winds long to play with your hair." Gibran believed it held humanity together with a divine property. He believed that unity with nature was a religious act and that, ideally, nature and humanity should be in a perfect symbiotic relationship.

2.2   Hybrid Literature

The Mahjar writers attempted to become acceptable to the white Americans whom they tried to impress by emulation, yet they were still concerned about losing their Arabic identity and their language. This resulted in hybridity, a blending of traditions. The Mahjar writers focused on spirituality, their Christian identities and geographical connection with the "Holy Land." They focused heavily on biblical language and parallels, seeking to distance themselves from Islam while making the "exotic" terrain of the Middle East a common motif in their writings (Majaj).

The melding of Eastern and Western literature produced free poetry styles, which were a definite break away from the metered styles of traditional Arabic poetry. Many of the Mahjar writers also adopted the modern philosophy of their new homeland. They simplified their native writing traditions in an attempt to make their work more understandable and accepted by a country that did not understand their native language. Many Arabic writers felt that they lived during a period of degeneration in Arabic literature, and that a new hybrid literature was being born, combining the best of both cultures' literature (Adegboyega). As Irfan Shahid notes, Gibran took part in bringing about the Renaissance of Arab literature and its impact on American Literature (5). Though Gibran is not fully accepted as a part of American literature, being excluded from the literary canon, he still influenced Mahjar writers to Americanize the genres of Arabic literature (6).

Mahjar literature had many characteristics of literature from the Romanticism style (see table 1). In comparing Mahjar literature to the characteristics of Romanticism, it is evident that their literature more closely relates to Romanticism than Realism, though there was a transition from the first to the latter at that period (see table 3).

Table 1 Characteristics of Mahjar literature

Characteristic	Explanation
Imaginary characters	Characters are not true-to-life; may be may be mystical
Static characters	Contrary to what is generally accepted as good literature, characters do not show development or growth over time
Characterization according to author's vision	Characterization is strongly based on the author's vision; description of imaginary characters
Imaginary and mystical universe	Universe is made to conform to writer's perception; may be mystical and definitely imaginary
Weak cause and effect	Events happen outside a cause/effect – it appears they happen independently
Formal language	Language conforms to accepted formal language of the geographical location in which the writer lives
Good is rewarded, evil punished	Good always wins out, evil always loses, contrary to what may actually happen in "real life"
Truths not revealed in text	Truths to be learned from the text is not directly revealed – reader must make interpretation
Plot revolves around crisis points	There is no strong plot – crises drive the telling of the "story"
Important points in plot include love, honor, and idealism	Though the story is imaginary, love, honor, and idealism were strong plot points
Dreams and visions foretell the future	Plot revealed through dreams of the "spiritually aware" to help the common population understand
Heavy use of description	Less action (plot) than a description of the world, society, and characters involved in telling the "story"

2.3   Arabic literary societies

The Mahjar writers banded together to form special literary societies to help spread their influence as writers and to ensure the preservation of their literature. These societies developed over a number of years, each with a different focus, but with the underlying purpose of spreading their writings throughout the "New World" in which they found themselves residing (Jafarov and Ibrahimovaf 195).

2.3.1 The Pen League

Formed in New York in 1920, the first of such societies in North America was The Pen League. It was initially formed in 1915, and later re-formed in 1920 by a new leader who was supported by a group of young Arab writers who had been closely aligned since 1911 (Jafarov and Ibrahimovaf 201).

An Arab-American newspaper published in 1912 became the official press for the Pen League. It provided important messages to the Arabic world from Arab-Americans and influenced many writers. Members of the Pen League published their works in the newspaper (Islam 144).

After the death of its founder in 1931 and the return in 1932 of some of its leaders to Lebanon, the Pen League was dissolved (Islam 144). One of the Mahjar writers, Gibran Khalil Gibran, playwright, writer, and artist, inspired many other writers. He was later recommended by George Bush to be honored with a memorial garden (Islam 144).

The Pen Leagues was the largest literary society among the Mahjar writers. It united writers who looked at literature with a new set of forms. They had very specific objectives and purposes for their union.

One of their objectives was a two-fold effort. They strove to preserve the traditional literature and literary styles of their homeland, while at the same time infusing their literature with new ideas. They advocated writing in the new simplified language that had developed over time in their new world in America. They tried to eliminate archaic Arabic language in their writings. Writing prose with intense feelings meant that the prose overshadowed poetry (Jafarov and Ibrahimovaf 202).

2.3.2   The Minerva society

The Minerva society, established in 1948, again in New York by an Egyptian writer, had similar goals to the Egyptian counterpart, Apollo. It was short-lived, dissolving after the death of its founder. It short life meant it had less impact on the Mahjar literature than other such societies, though it was populated by several important Arab writers (Jafarov and Ibrahimovaf   202).

2.3.3   The Maari society

The next society was the Maari Society. It started in South America in 1900, in spite of the slower development of Mahjar literature than that experienced in North America. This slower development was most likely due to the lack of education and the financial difficulties, and the lack of organization among these poorly educated Arabs. They published the first set of poems from these Mahjar writers. It became a national club of Arabs. They held meetings with readings, and frequent meetings occurred. They established a free school in which educated Arabs taught those less educated. It dissolved at the beginning of First World War (Jafarov and Ibrahimovaf   202).

2.3.4   The Syrian society

The Syrian Society came next, during the First World War. It was short-lived, lasting only two years, but influenced young Arabs nonetheless. It was Brazilian, founded by an Arab newspaper editor.

2.3.5   The al-Adab society

The al-Adab Society began in 1922 in Brazil. It contributed to Mahjar literature, and led to the publication and promotion of Arab literature in Brazil. The money recognized from the sale of the literature was used to educate and provide material needs to young Arabs. This one lasted until the 1960s. They writers participated in the annual "Mahrajan Sheir Ukazi," or the "Ukaz Poetry Festival," conducted at the urging of the al-Adab Society. (Jafarov and Ibrahimovaf   202).

2.3.6   The Literature society

The Literature Society, founded in 1949 in Buenos Aires by George Saydah, had as its main objective, the advancement of Arabic literature in America. It only lasted for two years until George Saydah returned to Lebanon (Jafarov and Ibrahimovaf 202).

2.3.7   The Andalusian society

Founded in 1933, in San Paulo, was a South American society, the Andalusian Society. It was bigger than the rest. The Republic of Turkey's President, Mustafa Kamal, impressed its founders. He gave credit to the President for developing a strong country as a valuable leader. He credited the people of Turkey as being intelligent. Its name came from the tradition of the Arabs to call Spain Andalusia. The literature from that area was rich, as was its culture, and melded the East and West (Jafarov and Ibrahimovaf 203).

Though both groups of writers longed for their homeland, their poems were different. Mahjar poets were more emotional and candid. They addressed the difficulties of migrant Arabs, including living conditions and their strong longing for their homeland. Their literature was considered to be just a continuation of the Andalusian literature, though they differed in that the Mahjar writers showed the inner person much more successfully (Islam 144).

The Andalusian Society had as its objectives to establish the "new world" and to spread the literature of both the Mahjar and the Middle East reciprocally. This society lasted until 1941, when the president of Brazil banned the all print done in a foreign language (Islam 144).

The seven societies each, in its own way, helped to further the Mahjar literature. Whether short-lived or longer, they contributed in preserving and furthering the rich heritage of this proud people (see table 2).

Table 2 Mahjar literary societies

Society Name	Dates	Focus
The Pen League	1920-1931	• Preserve their literary heritage while adopting new one • New, simplified language • Elimination of archaic Arabic language • Primarily prose with intense feelings
The Minerva Society	1948-1950	Patterned after the Egyptian society "Apollo"
The Maari Society	1900-1914	Encouraged young poets; conducted many meetings in which reading occurred
The Syrian Society	Lasted 2 yrs during WWI	Encouraged your writers; Founded by a newspaper editor in Brazil
The al-Adab Society	1922-1960s	Money earned from sale of works was used to fund education for young Arabs
The Literature Society	1949-1951	Main focus was to promote Arab literature in America
The Andalusian Society	1933-1965	Its main focus was to borrow from the rich literature of the Andalusian writers from the past and use it to meld east and west, while not getting involved in politics

2.4 Focus of Mahjar literature

The Mahjar writers assimilated the established literary focus of the "New World", while keeping true to their own cultural literature, melding a new literary focus in the process. They helped to join the East and West.

The Mahjar writers attempted to make themselves acceptable to the white Americans whom they tried to impress by emulation. They still were concerned about losing their Arabic identity and their language. This resulted in a blended genre. They focused on their Christian identities, their geographical bonus of the "Holy Land," and their spiritual natures. They heavily focused on biblical language and parallels, seeking to distance themselves for Islam and make the "exotic" common in their writings (Majaj).

Gibran summed up this aspect of influence by the western world and it literature when he wrote:

> If the meaning of beauty of thought requires the breaking
>
> of rulers, break it. If there is no known word to express
>
> your idea, borrow or invent one if syntax stands in the way
>
> of needed or useful expression, away with the syntax. (Majaj)

Additionally, this melding of eastern and western literature resulted in free poetry styles, a definite move from the metered styles of traditional Arabic poetry. Many also adopted the modern philosophy of their new homeland. They simplified their own native writings in an attempt to make it more understandable and accepted by a country that did not understand their native language. Though many Arabic writers felt that the time was a period of degeneration in Arabic literature, and new hybrid literature was born, combining the best of both cultures' literature (Adegboyega).

2.5   Extinction of Romanticism

Though officially, as a literary style, romanticism has ended, it has never really become extinct. Though other styles, such as Realism and Modernism, have overtaken it as a major movement, it is still a part of good literature. However, writers began to desire to share their views in a more practical, immediate way, doing so in a way that ignored the real problems. Romantics focused on individuals instead of society, addressing the individual imagination. As modernization progressed, the focus began to be on the problems faced by society, and Romantics did not do that (Rahn). Romanticism has unique themes and characteristics, many of which are still evident in modern literature, though many consider it no longer a major influence on literature. These characteristics are in direct contrast to Realism and Naturalism. However, their influence appears in both movements (Strickland).

Though the style of literature during the turn of the century was moving toward Realism and away from Romanticism, the influence of Romanticism has never fully died. The influence of this style was strongly evident in the Mahjar writers (see Table 3).

Table 3 Comparison of Mahjar literature to Romantic literature

Mahjar Characteristic	Romanticism Characteristic
Imaginary characters	Imaginative
Static characters	Static characters
Characterization according to author's vision	Strong characterization according to author's vision
Imaginary and mystical universe	Imaginary and mystical universe
Weak cause and effect	Weak cause and effect
Formal language	Formal language
Good is rewarded, evil punished	Good is rewarded, evil punished
Truths not revealed in text	Not evident
Plot revolves around crisis points	Plot revolves around crisis points
Important points in plot include love, honor, and idealism	Important points in plot include love, honor, and idealism
Dreams and visions foretell the future	Dreams and visions foretell the future
Heavy use of description	Heavy use of description

2.6   The advent of Realism

Realism saw its advent during the late nineteenth century. Several events helped usher in this era. One was the end of the Civil War. This led to the beginning of the Industrial Revolution. Immigration was on the rise, as was the middle class (Villarreal).

Character was the most important focus during the Realism movement in American Literature. Action and plot took second place. Writers explained characters by nature, social class, and their relationship to each other. Events are believable instead of sensational as in the Romantic period. Language was natural, not poetic. The tone could be comical, satirical, or more down-to-earth (Villarreal).

Realism led to Naturalism. Though Realism focused on technique, Naturalism related characters to their environments. They made it appear as if surroundings, heredity, instinct and chance controlled characters. Society and culture often controlled a character's obligations (Villarreal).

Works addressing the transition from Romanticism to American Realism and the impact both writers had on this transition is a focus. The impact of the transition from one era to the other, and the influence of the societal norms surrounding the writers at the time of producing these works is one point of examination. The marginalization of the writers, Gilman because of gender and Gibran because of race, will be compared in light of the time of this transition. Examination of the impact of this marginalization on their writing will be included.

At a lecture series at Georgetown, Shahid, as a guest lecturer, connected Gibran to the Renaissance of Arab literature and its impact on American Literature (5). Though Gibran was not fully accepted in the American Literature world, i.e. being excluded from the Canon, he still had a major impact is his leading of the Mahjar writers to Americanize the genres of Arabic literature (6).

2.7   Transcendentalist Influence on Gibran

In an 1842 lecture titled "The Transcendentalist," Ralph Waldo Emerson gave credence to a philosophical view that many in America saw as new. It was not new but rather a development in the Western philosophical tradition of idealism, which traced its roots back to Plato. The term "transcendentalism" was derived from the philosopher Immanuel Kant's *Critique of Pure Reason* (1798). For Kant, "transcendentalism" signified an idealism that could defeat John Locke's thesis that all human ideas are based upon and largely limited to sensuous experiences. Kant showed that there were *a priori* intuitions of time and space, and certain formative ideas, such as causality and existence, which did not arise through the senses, but which shaped sensuous experience. These intuitions of the mind were *a priori* or "transcendental forms" (Goodman 101-2). Popularizers of transcendentalism in the United States construed Kant's philosophy as an intellectual foundation for an expansive confidence in inborn human mental powers. They believed that miracles could result from an open mind and the power of the human imagination (Goodman 100).

Transcendentalism became a driving force in American literature in the half century before Gibran's time, with ideas popularized by such authors as Ralph Waldo Emerson. Though Gibran was not a self-proclaimed transcendentalist, the influence of Emerson and other transcendentalists is evident in his writings. "Emerson's persisting influence on late-nineteenth- and twentieth-century American writers is evident in astonishing permutations..." ("Ralph Waldo Emerson" 489).

Ahmad Y. Majdoubeh suggests that Emerson influenced Gibran's writing in two ways. First, Gibran used Emerson's works as a direct resource for some of his work. It was through Emerson's writings that Gibran became acquainted with Neo-Platonism and Buddhism (Majdoubeh 478). Although Emerson and Gibran were from dissimilar religious backgrounds, their most popular works show similar transcendentalist ideas about spirituality. Both Emerson's essay "Self-Reliance" and Gibran's *The Prophet* explore the relationship between the Self's search for an authentic way of life and a personally satisfying religion. Emerson says the true man should think of himself and his God as aspects of a transcendent divinity. In *The Prophet*, Gibran's al-Mustafa emphasizes the need for self-knowledge in making religious commitments. Gibran's characterization of religion as an aspect of individual development is similar to Emerson's (Bushrui).

Gibran's prophet al-Mustafa and Emerson's Self-Reliant man offer similar guidance on love and friendship (Bushrui). Both characters prefer solitude yet realize the importance of friends in life. Both characters understand that one must be true to oneself, and not copy friends.

Gibran, speaking through al-Mustafa, says, "If he [your friend] must know the ebb of your tide let him know its flood also" (Gibran 70). The Self-Reliant man had a similar commentary on friendship. He says, "If you can love me for what I am, we shall be happier.... If you are true but not in the same truth with me.... I will seek my own [companions]" (Emerson 543-544).

Emerson says the Self-Reliant man is one who knows goodness. However, for Emerson, good and bad are relative. Good is what is good for the Self-Reliant man; bad is what is wrong for him (Emerson 535). Similarly, Gibran's al-Mustafa says, "You are good when you are one with yourself." However, he says, doing good or not-good things is not what makes you evil or bad (75).

Both the Self-Reliant man and al-Mustafa believe prayers should be directed toward thinking about one's life, not asking God for things. The Self-Reliant man says prayer is "the contemplation of the facts of life" (Emerson 545). Al-Mustafa similarly says prayer is "...the expansion of yourself into the living ether..." (78). Both authors recommend prayer as a daily activity. The Self-Reliant man, for example, says, "As soon as the man is at one with God, he will not beg. He will then see prayer in all action" (Emerson 545). Al-Mustafa says, "God listens not to your words save when He Himself utters them through your lips" (81). Speaking your prayers, according to them, is God saying His words through your lips.

According to *The Prophet*, God is in everything, from nature to the sphere of the entire earth. Al-Mustafa says, "You are a breath in God's sphere and a leaf in God's forest..." (60). He says that religion is everything humans do and in everything around us. Al-Mustafa says, "Your daily life is your temple and your religion" (91). Al-Mustafa teaches that worship continues as long as one loves life. In like manner, the Self-Reliant man believes that everything in life is a part of a person's religion. According to both authors, there is no life apart from religion, and no religion apart from life. The Self-Reliant man says that all things are "one with them, and proceeds obviously from the same source whence their life and being also proceed [God]" (Emerson 540).

Although Emerson's transcendentalist ideas deeply influenced Gibran, it is clear in comparing "Self-Reliance" and *The Prophet* that the two hold different views of the past. Al-Mustafa says, "let to-day embrace the past with remembrance" (74) while Emerson shows that he minimizes the focus on the past. He has the Self-Reliant man negate the importance of the past above the present when he says, "history is an impertinence and an injury, if it be anything more than a cheerful apologue or parable of my being and becoming" (Emerson 541).

In addition to the transcendentalist focus of *The Prophet*, the reader can see the influence of Biblical literature, Christian and Sufi mysticism, Buddhism, and Hinduism on Gibran's most famous work (Mcharek). Gibran's imagery is based primarily upon nature; he frequently compares the natural and the human worlds. In his poetry, he recognized the symbols of nature, depicting a life promoting the kinship of all men and borrowing from nature symbols for both the emotional and intellectual messages of his poetry. He touted the sanctity that nature held and stressed a duty to protect, sanctify, and celebrate nature and to learn from and commune with it.

One great difference from traditional Arabic literature was in Gibran's depiction of nature. In Arabic literature, nature was depicted as something to be contended with, while Gibran viewed it as having a life of its own. He endowed it with spiritual, emotional, and intellectual properties: "Forget not that the earth delights to feel your bare feet and the winds long to play with your hair." He believed it held humanity together with a divine property. He believed that unity with nature was a religious act. He believed nature and humanity to be in a perfect symbiotic relationship. He advocates its use in poetry and art, and exhibits the influence of such nature poets as Wordsworth, Keats and

Blake, and of American transcendentalists such as Emerson, Thoreau and Whitman (Bushrui).

Gibran showed a preoccupation with India and Hindu scriptures, which was usually attributed to American transcendentalists, but there was another potential influence, the Indian poet-philosopher, Rabindranath Tagore. Though Gibran did not learn any Indian language, he may well have drawn inspiration from this source as well as from the American transcendentalists (Datta).

It is quite apparent from Thoreau's works that he had an influence on Gibran's thinking when he acts as a mediator between man and nature and presents them as a prophetic entity. His main desire was to predict a new dawn for humanity, whether it be Eden or New Jerusalem, and encourage them to be ready for it. The promise of resurrection was a promise of paradise when man was ready for it (El-Hage). Blake influenced Gibran in seeing imagination as the only creator, and Emerson taught him that the "visible revealed the invisible." Gibran believed that both the self and nature were the source of true life and happiness for man, but he had to choose one over the other. He often showed harmony between man and nature, but also showed at times that the self emerged superior to nature. He was seeking God, not nature, but often sought the Divine through nature (El-Hage).

Gibran sought God throughout his life, but it was not always easy to understand his beliefs about the relationship between God-Man-Nature. He wanted to believe in a perfect God, but to him this meant continuous growth. He rejected a sense of stasis and stagnation. After *The Prophet*, Gibran, for the first time enjoyed the complete harmony and unity for which he had always longed but had never previously enjoyed. His philosophy, like Blake's, taught the hope of resurrection, infinite peace, and redemption (El-Hage).

American transcendentalists such as Walt Whitman, Ralph Waldo Emerson, and Henry David Thoreau made a major impact on Gibran's writings. He embraced their ideas, as is seen in their influence on his works. He adopted their ideas about reincarnation, and the individual self as an imitation one strives to grow into. He believed in the progress of human beings into a divine world. He believed in the metaphysical realm as a way to understand the higher life an individual has available in this world. Another strong influence upon Gibran and his religious beliefs were Friedrich Nietzsche and William Blake, who caused him to question his religion and the role of priests. He never, however, questioned that there was a God (Bushrui).

2.8 Abdu'l-Baha

Almost all readers of *The Prophet* are curious about its inspiration. They wonder if there was an actual prophet from which the book draws its inspiration – a holy man as al-Mustafa was depicted. If so, who was this man, and how can we find more of his teachings, they ask. Others wonder if the poet William Blake provided the major inspiration for this character. Some few even believe the inspiration came from the transcendentalists Emerson and Thoreau. There are many other suggestions people have made as to the possible influence. One often overlooked is Abdu'l-Baha, the eldest son of Bahá'u'lláh, the founder of the Bahá'í Faith. After meeting this person, Gibran stated, "He is a very great man. He is complete. There are worlds in his soul...." He also confessed to a colleague that he had "seen the Unseen, and been filled" (Bushrui and Jenkins 126).

Soon after this meeting and the ensuing statements, Gibran began his writing on a new work, *The Counsels*, which later became titled *The Prophet*. He stated to others, friends of his, that he had worked on this piece since 1912 when he first got an idea for the motif of an "Island God" who was exiled to an island (Bushrui and Jenkins 165).

There is some agreement that Gibran based his name for the exiled prophet al-Mustafa upon the name Al-Mustapha, which means in Arabic, The Chosen One, and on Abdu'l-Baha, by changing consonants to mimic the name. When Abdu'l-Baha visited New York, citizens sought the counsel of his wisdom.

Similarly, Gibran had as his overall plot in *The Prophet* the clamoring of citizens for the wisdom of al-Mustafa. Villagers referred to al-Mustafa as "the Master" just as Gibran had heard the Baha'i address Abdu'l-Baha. He followed by sharing, through al-Mustafa, the wisdom of Baha'i teachings:

> You have been told also that life is darkness, and in your weariness you echo what was said by the weary.
>
> And I say that life is indeed darkness save when there is urge,
>
> And all urge is blind save when there is knowledge.
>
> And all knowledge is vain save when there is work,
>
> And all work is empty save when there is love;
>
> And when you work with love you bind yourself to yourself, and to one another, and to God

("Work")

To compare, from the *Tablets of Baha'u'llah*, p. 26:

> It is enjoined upon every one of you to engage in some form of occupation, such as crafts, trades and the like. We have graciously exalted your engagement in such work to the rank of worship unto God, the True One. Ponder ye in your hearts the grace and the blessings of God and render thanks unto Him at eventide and at dawn. Waste not your time in idleness and sloth. Occupy yourselves with that which profiteth yourselves and others. Thus hath it been decreed in this Tablet from whose horizon the day-star of wisdom and utterance shineth resplendent....
>
> When anyone occupieth himself in a craft or trade, such occupation itself is regarded in the estimation of God as an act of worship; and this is naught but a token of His infinite and all-pervasive bounty.

(Langness)

Gibran used his talent as a writer to invite individuals to contemplate their dreams and visions. He had the uncanny talent to visualize the spiritual, which was considered by many to be above the normal (Ganaie 92).

Gibran was a mystic of a sort, if we accept the definition of a mystic loosely, taking it out of the realm of the holy or spiritual. The definition of a mystic is one who has had an abnormal experience on a personal level. His wisdom of the world around him was abnormal, or mystic. He tries to help others understand his experiences in order to see past the everyday world experiences (Ganaie 78). Gibran was concerned with the tension between body and soul. He believed the soul defined a man. He strove to help people realize the divine. He believed firmly in imagination, believing God and man shared it. He believed man reaches perfection because God is in everything. He did believe that God is transcendental, but also believed that nature and the physical is the key to understanding the relationship between God and Self. He also believed in the harmony between one's body and soul, and that each one is somewhat of a prophet. He felt strongly the responsibility to guide people to see and understand their inner self (Ganaie 90).

3   Critical Analysis of The Prophet

The Prophet is considered the most important work by Gibran. It is composed in the form of prose poems, twenty-eight in number, each individually complete. Each poem provides Gibran's view on some aspect of life or some problem that man might face. His views on each issue, if followed, would lead his readers to a utopian existence. Through fiction Gibran presents a work that teaches life lessons through the character of al-Mustafa, who acts as a prophet and teacher, exploring issues that Gibran believes are important in a culture. According to Farsi, "Gibran took on a fictional persona to deliver critical insights of the modern age" (346). Gibran draws from all religions when staging al-Mustafa's teachings. Al-Mustafa's teachings guide his followers as well as the world all over to form a concept of God that is both social and moral. His messages are friendly words of encouragement. Gibran appears to be attempting to overcome barriers between East and West on conflicting cultural and human issues (Buck, 2010; Acocella, 2008).

Written in the manner of prophecies, the prose poems of *The Prophet* reflect significantly on love, life, and families. They represent Gibran's views on important life issues, although the prophet, al-Mustafa, is the speaker who is giving the advice. The poems consist of the narrator's replies in answer to questions posed by residents of the land, asked when he was preparing to go back to his homeland, all describing a utopian universe (Ganaie 80). Gibran's fictional country and the city of Orphalese lend credibility to his philosophies, although they were not totally grounded in the culture of his time.

The language that Gibran uses for his narrator indicates that he believes that universal love and unity are healing powers. Gibran believed that a man existed in his soul and in his body. He believed that God moved in a man's mind. His ideology appealed to the world at his time, and still today continues to appeal to a wide audience. *The Prophet* is the second largest selling book in the world. The Bible is the only book that surpasses it (Ganaie 90).

Al-Mustafa is about to begin a journey to his native homeland. He has been away for years and is excited to get to go home, but is nostalgic about leaving the homeland he has adopted as his own for a dozen years. He agrees to answer the questions of those asking him, partially in an attempt to delay his departure. Nevertheless, the ship is coming and ultimately he must leave after relating words of wisdom for the people for guidance after he is gone (Ganaie 90). Gibran uses personification to refer to the abstract noun "love." He refers to love as *he, his,* and *him.* He declares and shows evidence to the people that pure love frees and purifies their souls. He shows a progression in his teachings, from a fear of God to a love of God and ideal worship (Ganaie 90). Gibran drew on his Eastern culture the belief he evinces in the philosophy of God as a spirit in all parts of the universe. The language in *The Prophet* promotes the idea of unity in diversity and the healing power of love and unity (Bushrui 68). Irwin quotes the French sculptor Auguste Rodin as saying that Gibran was "the Blake of the 20th century" (1).

In his attempt the correct the negative aspects of Western and Eastern society, Gibran presented a philosophical and religious approach. In commentary on what discourse entails and how it enlightens one, John S. Dryzek explains it as a "shared way of apprehending the world. Embedded in language, it enables those who subscribe to it to interpret bits of information and put them together into coherent stories or accounts. Each discourse rests on assumptions, judgments, and contentions that provide the basic terms for analysis, debates, agreements, and disagreements" (8).

In trying to explain how Gibran represents the world in *The Prophet*, Al-Khazaji, Fahmi, Abdullah and Wong look at several issues, as follows. An examination of these issues enables one to understand the problems that Gibran, and the world he wrote about, faced at the time. These issues had a great influence on

Gibran's writings as he attempted to make sense of them for himself and his audiences (Al-Khazaji, et al.).

3.1 Ethically and Morally Corrupt World

In *Up the Line to Death: The War Poets 1914-1918* (1964), editor Brian Gardner says that the poets of the early 20th century "found a brotherhood that transcended the barriers of class, strong at the time; of religion, of race, of every facet of society." Gibran looks for this same sense of bonding in humanity, regardless of religion, race, or politics (Al-Khazaji, et al.). In Gibran's mind, the whole world was deformed, and he wanted to teach people to release themselves from the evil that resulted after WWI, which had led to psychological and spiritual violence. This era was considered by historians of the time to be the most corrupt time in history, both morally and ethically. Declining social values were seen as a major characteristic of individuals of that time in which Gibran was writing. Thus, Gibran, in *The Prophet*, attempts to instruct people in the way life should be in reality in all its aspects. He teaches ethics based on certain religious tenets. In addition, Gibran teaches the people certain mores of society, based on the existing morality of the time. He did not teach these mores and ethics for any desire for political or other power, as some priests and politicians did, but intended, instead, to strengthen social stability, bring peace to society, and to help develop a life style of spirituality (Al-Khazaji, et al.).

In analyzing the different aspects of *The Prophet*, it is evident that the foremost value throughout is love. The first subsection is actually "Love," being the main point – the foremost point of departure throughout life and peace.

> All these things shall love do unto you that you may know the secrets of your heart, and in that knowledge become a fragment of Life's heart.

> But if in your fear you would seek only love's peace and love's pleasure.

Then it is better for you that you cover your nakedness and pass out of love's threshing-floor,

Into the seasonless world where you shall laugh, but not all of your laughter, and weep, but not all of your tears.

("Love")

This passage gives evidence that Gibran sees morality as unstable with his statement of "cover your nakedness" and "seasonless world" where moral instability and dissatisfaction with one's life is evidenced as only a marginal reflection on ethics (Al-Khazaji, et al.). Some critics have likened Gibran to William Blake, both being social reformers and prophets encouraging consciousness, rising beyond the current cultural beliefs (Al-Khazaji, et al.). In evaluating Gibran's works, Ludescher claims:

Gibran's early works depict a world in which the transcendent power of Nature is contrasted with the innate corruption of human society. For Gibran, Nature is both a living spiritualized being and a manifestation of God's universal law. Although humans in their natural state are pure and uncorrupted, they will only return to God and achieve their divine nature after they have evolved through the course of many lives on earth. (Ludescher 113)

Gibran actually drew many of his creative ideas from religion. The world at the end of the nineteenth century was corrupt, ethically and morally, and there was considerable religious conflict. Gibran was believed to use this form of writing against those who would use religious conflict for their own means. His Arabic writings, according to Hawi, were many times used to convey Gibran's strong belief and following of religious matters (141).

3.2   Love-Impoverished World

The people of Orphalese only realize the existence of love when they learn of it from al-Mustafa. They recognize their love toward al-Mustafa, declaring their love but saying it has previously been hidden and silent. They say, "Much have we loved you. But speechless was our love, and with veils has it been veiled ("The Coming of the Ship").

Gibran used his character al-Mustafa to teach his readers about an ideal love, uncorrupted, and about truth. He did not teach of individual love but of collective love between all peoples. Al-Mustafa speaks to his audience about living and acting as lovers in the world. Gibran understood the insufficiency of love in Orphalese, as he showed through al-Mustafa's words.

> When love beckons to you follow him,
>
> Though his ways are hard and steep.
>
> And when his wings enfold you yield to him,
>
> Though the sword hidden among his pinions may wound you.
>
> And when he speaks to you believe in him.
>
> ("Love").

Gibran shows his belief in love being a source of freedom to the soul and that it purifies it. He believes that love is in most human activities, using it sixty-four times in the text of *The Prophet*.

He attempts to show that love brings knowledge and moral assurance. He shows a progressive change from fear of God to love of Him in the ideal worship of the people.

Gibran also appeals to the love of nature, in both *The Prophet* and other works, appealing to simplicity of life since all civilization is a part of the corruption and misuse of nature, considering nature divine (Al-Khazaji, et al.).

3.2.1 Complexity of Life and the Materialistic World

Gibran shows his dissatisfaction with the complexity of life and the striving for achievements to the exclusion of spirituality. Gibran believed that nature had a life of its own, spiritually, emotionally, and intellectually, binding man to man. He appeals to environmentalists as he appeals to all to respect nature and not to destroy it. Gibran rejected materialism and supported helpfulness among all humanity. He listened to the spiritual by attending to people, nature, and the soul. Bushrui and Jemkins claim that "[i]n all his work he [Gibran] expressed the deep-felt desire of men and women for a kind of spiritual life that renders the material world meaningful and imbues it with dignity" (1).

3.2.2 Egotism and Dominate World

In texts on marriage, children, and friendship, Gibran mentions such negative experiences as emotional abandonment, self-importance and pride, and dominating behavior. In each, Gibran expresses discomfort with the corruption of what he considers a reasonable distance between spouses, the gap between parents and children, and the phoniness between friends. An example of his views on marriage is being together but not possessing or dominating the other. His views on the sanctity of marriage and the idea of being together until death are summarized here:

> You were born together, and together you shall be forevermore.
>
> You shall be together when white wings of death scatter your days.
>
> ("Marriage")

On individuality in marriage the Prophet says:

> But let there be spaces in your togetherness,
>
> And let the winds of the heavens dance between you.
>
> Love one another but make not a bond of love:
>
> Let it rather be a moving sea between the shores of your souls.
>
> Fill each other's cup but drink not from one cup.
>
> Give one another of your bread but eat not from the same loaf.
>
> ("Marriage")

Gibran uses the following imperative verbs to encourage people to avoid egotism: love, fill, give, sing, dance, and stand together. He criticizes the misunderstanding about proper parental care, but helps to coin the idea that children are our future.

Your children are not your children.

They are the sons and daughters of Life's longing for itself.

They come through you but not from you,

And though they are with you, yet they belong not to you.

("Children")

We also see how Gibran presents family life and the parental treatment of children when he discourages parents from ruling over their children and forcing them to follow their example, and trying to shape the children's world.

You may strive to be like them, but seek not to make them like you.

For life goes not backward nor tarries with yesterday.

("Children")

On friendship, Gibran states that friendship can involve warmth, knowledge, and peace. It also allows for laughter and joy. When asked about friendship, al-Mustafa says:

Your friend is your needs answered.

He is your field which you sow with love and reap with thanksgiving.

And he is your board and your fireside.

For you come to him with your hunger, and you seek him for peace.

When your friend speaks his mind you fear not the "nay" in your own mind, nor do you withhold the "ay."

("Friendship")

Gibran is, however, a recluse, avoiding the sorrows and perversions of the world. Readers of *The Prophet* consider it theologically sound and a guide to reforming the world. Gibran was a social reformer and an anthropomorphic prophet, as is mentioned in some verses in texts as follows:

Prophet of God, in quest for the uttermost, long have you searched the distances for your ship.

("The Coming of the Ship")

For the master spirit of the earth shall not sleep peacefully upon the wind till the needs of the least of you are satisfied.

("Buying and Selling")

3.2.3   Injustice and Oppression

It is impossible to ignore Gibran's political ideas, as environmental, political and social concerns influenced his creativity in his works. His genius and emotions also helped shaped his creativity, based on his concerns. He does not state political views directly, but as allegories, encouraging reform in both church and state. He rejects strict laws and authoritarian government action in the attempt to force strict obedience.

But to whom life is a rock, and the law a chisel with which they would carve it in their own likeness?

But you who walk facing the sun, what images drawn on the earth can hold you? ("Laws")

And how shall you rise beyond your days and nights unless you break the chains which you at the dawn of your understanding have fastened around your noon hour?

("Freedom")

Many factors in Gibran's life influenced his ideology and his outlook on life. These factors included Ottoman colonization of his Arab country and the poverty, disease and destitution he suffered in America. These factors shaped his view of the world around him. One example is his idea of the word *freedom*. He says, in *The Prophet*, about freedom:

At the city gate and by your fireside I have seen you prostrate yourself and worship your own freedom,

Even as slaves humble themselves before a tyrant and praise him
though he slays them.

("Freedom")

Gibran feels that people interpret freedom as a weapon, not as an
aspiration toward which they should strive. He believed societies
only became free when they saw freedom as a tangible concept.
Ludescher states that "Gibran was not interested in reforming the
corrupt social system by replacing oppressive laws with progressive ones, but instead was advocating absolute freedom" (114).

> You shall be free indeed when your days are not without a care
> nor your nights without a want and a grief,
>
> But rather when these things girdle your life and yet you rise
> above them naked and unbound.

("Freedom")

Gibran seeks justice with social solidarity by glorifying morality.

> And the robbed is not blameless in being robbed.
>
> The righteous is not innocent of the deeds of the wicked,
>
> And the white-handed is not clean in the doings of the felon.

("Crime and Punishment")

Gibran recognizes justice as the legislation of the Lord, not as the
laws of man. Politicians and leaders, according to Gibran, often
are not aware whether their rules are helpful or harmful to society.
Analysts agree with Ludescher when he says, "Gibran challenges
the arbitrary injustices of the legal system, whose manmade laws
are frequently in conflict with the more enduring and just laws of
nature" (112).

> Is not remorse the justice which is administered by that very law
> which you would fain serve?

Yet you cannot lay remorse upon the innocent nor lift it from the heart of the guilty.

("Crime and Punishment")

If it is an unjust law you would abolish, that law was written with your own hand upon your own forehead.

("Freedom")

Gibran believed that manmade laws represent hypocrisy, despotism and persecution. Al-Mustafa proclaims:

You delight in laying down laws,

Yet you delight more in breaking them.

("Laws")

Gibran condemns hypocrisy and speaks about moral law and the religious aspects of law. On questioning man's law, Gibran asks rhetorical questions:

What man's law shall bind you if you break your yoke but upon no man's prison door?

What laws shall you fear if you dance but stumble against no man's iron chains?

("Laws")

Gibran consistently addressed the need for freedom, as he had a strong desire to promote spiritual movement.

Probably because Gibran belonged to two different cultures, he shows a sense of self-alienation, injustice, and social responsibility. This is especially noticeable at both the beginning and the ending of the book. Al-Mustafa speaks of this when the ship arrives and again at the end when he is about to leave.

How shall I go in peace and without sorrow? Nay, not without a wound in the spirit shall I leave this city.

Long were the days of pain I have spent within its walls, and long were the nights of aloneness; and who can depart from his pain and his aloneness without regret?

("The Coming of the Ship")

The silence of aloneness reveals to their eyes their naked selves and they would escape.

("Talking")

These feelings of isolation and alienation are evident when al-Mustafa wants to leave Orphalese, even though he will be returning to his homeland.

And some of you have called me aloof, and drunk with my own aloneness,

And you have said: "He holds council with the trees of the forest, but not

with men.

"He sits alone on hill-tops and looks down upon our city."

True it is that I have climbed the hills and walked in remote places.

How could I have seen you save from a great height or a great distance?

How can one be indeed near unless he be far?

("The Farewell")

In *The Prophet*, the idea of man as the image of God is pervasive in the text. Gibran abhors the multiplicity of religions. Due to the multiplicity of religions, people have different views regarding worship and rituals, which often leads to conflict, something that is abhorrent to Gibran. This multiplicity in religious ideas often leads to conflict between nations. Gibran's beliefs are in agreement with all religions that support an everlasting spirit.

And then he assigns you to his sacred fire, that you may become sacred bread for God's sacred feast.

("Love")

Gibran was in support of unity among religions. He proposed that God is everywhere, that man dwells in God's heart, and that all is Godly. He believed each person had an undefiled part of God as the self.

When you love you should not say, "God is in my heart," but rather, I am in the heart of God."

("Love")

Aye, you shall be together even in the silent memory of God.

("Marriage")

And when you work with love you bind yourself to yourself, and to one another, and to God.

("Work")

God listens not to your words save when He Himself utters them through your lips.

("Prayer")

Al-Mustafa, the central character in *The Prophet*, speaks throughout the book about the unity of religions. All the characters in the book help to enhance Gibran's views in focus of the questions that were important to them. The moral values and al-Mustafa's teachings on many issues of life point toward a utopian city, as the world that Gibran desires and depicts through al-Mustafa is not yet in existence. The principles in the message taught draw from all religions, absolving dogmatism and embracing the pure parts of those religions, namely love, unity, and understanding. Al-Mustafa's teachings encourage all to embrace a moral conception of God as love (Al-Khazaji, et al.).

4 The Prophet and Four Institutions of Culture

To examine a culture, it is important to define what culture means and to be able to identify the culture(s) in question. Since literature affects culture and culture in turn affects literature, the study of literature grants admission to the history, habits and cherished ideals of the group. Conversely, an examination of a culture helps one to understand the literature of that culture. One definition of culture is that it constitutes the sets of differences in a society, in particular where they affect the values of the group (Maznevski, et al. 276). Cultural values are learned by interacting with the members of a social group, most specifically with the family. Upon a person's birth, the institutions of a culture are already in place – things such as language, politics, education, and family structures. Over a person's lifetime, however, these institutions may change. As children grow, they learn the accepted response to situations based on the cultural values that surround them. However, in order to survive, the young must also learn to change with their culture (Thomas and Peterson 23).

There are several institutions that comprise a culture. The four institutions under discussion in this paper are among the most fundamental social structures: family, education, religion, and politics. The values, objectives and objects of a culture are a collective work, produced by the bond of people with each other. To fully understand culture, one must view it as not simple collective works but need to understand how the social products are formed from the societal changes surrounding their development (McNeely 4). Over time, a culture maintains those institutions that support it, and eliminates those that are detrimental. Thus, culture is not static at all, but dynamic, in order to maintain the stability of the group (Thomas and Peterson 27). Changes encountered in a society bring about the development of different institutions in a culture. Though many tend to interpret such changes as problems, they really lead to the progression of cultural institutions (McNeely 3). Gibran speaks to each of these aspects of culture in *The Prophet*. He emphasizes the importance of the four institutions but also stresses the importance of maintaining individuality.

4.1 Family

In speaking of marriage, which relates to his views of family, Gibran's Prophet tells the interested group around him:

> Fill each other's cup but drink not from one cup.
>
> Give one another of your bread but eat not from the same loaf.

("Marriage")

The common theme here is twofold. It is the instruction not to allow the marriage relationship to define your life, and, secondly, that pure love goes beyond oneself. There is enjoyment in individual pursuits as well. The whole purpose of unity is to strengthen each other in the partnership.

A common theme in *The Prophet* is revealed when al-Mustafa speaks about children:

> Give your hearts, but not into each other's keeping.
>
> For only the hand of Life can contain your hearts.

("Marriage")

On love, which is a part of family relationships, Gibran says:

> Love gives naught but itself and takes naught but from itself.
>
> Love possesses not nor would it be possessed;
>
> For love is sufficient unto love.

("Love")

Gibran seems to be saying that though the family relationship is vital, it is not the all-encompassing relationship. He seems to be saying that one needs to maintain individuality.

> Ay, you shall be together even in the silent memory of God.
>
> But let there be spaces in your togetherness,
>
> And let the winds of the heavens dance between you.

("Marriage")

Gibran expounds on children, saying thus:

> Your children are not your children.
>
> They are the sons and daughters of Life's longing for itself.
>
> They come through you but not from you,
>
> And though they are with you yet they belong not to you.

("Children")

With his comments we see that Gibran is saying that even in marriage as a parent, each person is to remain an individual. There seems to be even more distance between parent and child, he appears to say, than the distance between the individuals of a couple. However, even within a couple, individuality must be maintained.

4.2   Education

Al-Mustafa reveals his thoughts on education when he tells the crowd that if one is wise, he does not try to lead you to his idea of learning, but rather leads you to your own interests

> If he is indeed wise he does not bid you enter the house of his wisdom, but rather leads you to the threshold of your own mind.

("Teaching")

The whole city of Orphalese in *The Prophet* had access to the same knowledge as al-Mustafa.

> People of Orphalese, of what can I speak save of that which is even now moving your souls?
>
> ("The Coming of the Ship")

This was because they had an interest in learning all of which al-Mustafa had knowledge. If not, they would not have been able to be taught.

> No man can reveal to you aught but that which already lies half asleep in the dawning of your knowledge
>
> ("Teaching")

4.3   Religion

Gibran saw religion in a different light than his culture at the time. He did not see religion as a battle between Good and Evil. Al-Mustafa explains religion to his followers:

> Your daily life is your temple and our religion.
>
> Whenever you enter into it take with you your all.
>
> Take the plough and the forge and the mallet and the lute,
>
> The things you have fashioned in necessity or for delight.
>
> ("Religion")

On prayer, Gibran tells his audience:

> You pray in your distress and in your need; would that you might pray also in the fullness of your joy and in your days of abundance.
>
> For what is prayer but the expansion of yourself into the living ether?
>
> And if it is for your comfort to pour your darkness into space, it is also for your delight to pour forth the dawning of your heart
>
> ("Prayer")

Thus Gibran depicts a loving, benevolent God, who desires to communicate with his followers and to bring good to them, in place of the common perception of a stern and punishing God.

4.4 Love of country

Gibran sets his writing in a distant city, Orphalese. He shows the love that al-Mustafa has for his homeland and for the land where he dwells. He teaches the people about how to view the land and its laws. Al-Mustafa instructs his people to accept their laws. They can only live in peace, he instructs them, if they do not disregard the laws that had formed them.

> You delight in laying down laws,
>
> Yet you delight more in breaking them.
>
> ("Laws")

> If it is an unjust law you would abolish, that law was written with your own hand upon your own forehead.
>
> You cannot erase it by burning your law books nor by washing the foreheads of your judges, though you pour the sea upon them
>
> ("Freedom")

Gibran shows his philosophy on patriotism and love of country when he has al-Mustafa launch into a monologue about his excitement and his remorse when he spies the ship that is coming to get him to take him to his homeland. Al-Mustafa says:

> How shall I go in peace and without sorrow? Nay, not without a wound in the spirit shall I leave this city.
>
> Long were the days of pain I have spent within its walls, and long were the nights of aloneness; and who can depart from his pain and his aloneness without regret?
>
> ("The Coming of the Ship")

5   Charlotte Perkins Gilman: Life and Work

Charlotte Gilman was born Charlotte Anna Perkins on July 3, 1860, in Hartford, Connecticut. She was the great niece of Harriet Beecher Stowe, author of *Uncle Tom's Cabin*. Gilman's father abandoned the family when she was a child. She came of age in a country where women eventually gained the vote but remained far from equal to men.

Prior to the Civil War women were venturing into educational options but had access to several colleges by the time of the Civil War. After the War, the founding of several women's colleges was at least in part due to Gilman's legacy. This led to a new breed of women who demanded their place in the workforce and recognition for their accomplishments (Lane 14). By the end of the nineteenth century, women had begun experiencing vocational and educational options that were previously unavailable to them. They realized they could have options outside the common beliefs of the culture in that time.

In Gilman's world, society was patriarchal. Women's purpose in life was caring for a husband, children, and the home (Lane 13). Gilman experienced her first marriage to Walter Stetson in 1884 and care of their infant daughter as miserably confining. "The Yellow Wallpaper" (1892), Gilman's autobiographical and most popular fictional work, details the descent into mental illness of a woman kept locked up for total rest in a room under the care of her physician-husband. A later marriage to George Houghton Gilman in 1900 proved more compatible with Gilman's scholarly and literary ambitions (Beekman).

In her life and her work, Gilman attempted to redefine the submissive role of women. She envisioned a well-educated person who was economically self-sufficient and politically active. In *Herland*, the women characters displayed these traits (De Simone). Gilman was a prolific writer. Some of her feminist works included: *A

Woman's Utopia; *Concerning Children, The Home*, and *Human Work*; *The Home: Its Work and Influence*; *A Garden of Babies*; *The Beauty of the Block*; and *Maidstone Comfort* (Kessler 64-66). Gilman's utopian writings include the following:

Moving the Mountain depicted what the world would be like if changed to suit women. It was not one of her best works, but did present this world through the eyes of a man, in an attempt to validate such a world (Kessler 63). *What Diantha Did* commented on what a woman needs to contribute to a society that is monogamous and supported by a capitalist society (Kessler 63-64). *Her Memories*, published in Gilman's magazine *The Forerunner*. This was an account by an unnamed male who recounted his female companion's memories about her life in a utopian community. The children were cared for in community care centers. Occupants received meals prepared and delivered to them by others (Kessler 64).

The utopian nature of the fictional *Herland* makes Gilman's feminist ideals seem believable. In order to promote her innovative sociological views, Gilman found it necessary to present them in a fictionalized context, because society at the time would not accept a nonfiction work by a woman promoting such ideas (Salinas). Gilman's fictional women were able to fend for themselves in a society independent of men. She describes a utopian community totally run and run well by a society of women. No men are a part of this society. This was in total dissonance with the conditions of Gilman's world at the time.

Published in 1915, when women were beginning to question their traditional role as helpmate of man, *Herland* depicts a separatist feminist utopia (Cavataro 1). Gilman was able to write literature from her own experience to address the subject of women's oppression (Baumgartner 5). With *Herland*, Gilman first ventured into the realm of feminism, or questioning of the place to which women were relegated by the male population and indeed the entire society. Later works were even believed to depict a Utopian society if women were given proper significance, and the focus were on human values, not masculine ones (Kamal 396).

Gilman has been termed a poet, a preacher, an iconoclast, and a social theoretician. She addressed the question of women's rights in her written work, as well as in her personal life. In religion, Gilman was a humanist, who worked for the betterment of the human race (Allen 29). Before her death, Gilman stated she was not interested in personal immortality. She said she was only interested in Humanity (the capital H was hers) and that she was content with God (Allen 30). Echoing the transcendentalists, Gilman believed she was a vital part of God, and that she was a vessel for divine energy. She drew strength from her personal mysticism more than anything else (Allen 35). After being diagnosed with inoperable breast cancer in 1932, Gilman died of an intentional overdose of chloroform on August 17, 1935.

5.1   Utopianism

Utopia and Utopian refer to a society that enjoys perfect harmony. This perfection in harmony includes both harmony among individuals as well as peace with one's self and with God or a supernatural spiritual being. These terms further indicate a condition that is highly improbable or unattainable. Both words are used interchangeably to indicate any idea that is beyond the normally expected or beyond the attainable (Utopianism).

The idea of utopia often involves a longing for a time in the far past when things are remember as being void of evil and everybody and everything works together in harmony. It generally involves simplicity, with few wants and needs and complete satisfaction with the fulfillment of current needs. There is the perception of a simple, natural harmony, one disparaged by traditional thoughts (Utopianism).

Utopianism is the seeking of a harmony that is apart from a natural setting. Any such harmony experienced is thought to happen only in a perfect society, one in which everyone strives to live. The harmony results from the common beliefs of humanity, not just the ramblings of a unique, innovative thinker (Utopianism).

Though utopia names a perfect, harmonious existence, it is not just one standard idea. There are a number of such ideas, varying by the thinker presenting the idea, each with his own idea of harmony and perfection (Utopianism).

Great social change often results from the expression by a writer in reference to utopia. Though not always the cause of change, normally the utopian writings have had a big impact on such changes due to its impact on the conscience of a society (Utopianism).

An added benefit of the writings of utopian thinkers is that it leads to an enhanced vision of human possibility, encouraging dreams and visions of a better world. These writings pinpoint the idea that no society enjoys the full potential of humanity. Each one develops certain ideas and suppresses others. Though promoting the idea of perfection, utopian literature also helps to make a society aware that there is much more to enjoy in life than what is currently being enjoyed. These writers must characterize their writings in a unique way, excluding some ideas and simplifying others for the comprehension of the common society (Utopianism).

5.2 Commonalities within four institutions of culture

There are several accepted institutions of a culture as determined by sociologists and other scientists. For the purpose of this study, the examination and comparison addressed only four of the disciplines. Examining the four institutions are compared for their commonalities (see table 4).

Table 4 Comparison of four institutions

	Family	Education	Religion	Patriotism
Gibran	Love between man and woman encouraged; children are an extension of parents, but love for them is secondary to love between the parents.	To teach another, address their interests and ideas, do not try to force them to accept yours.	Rejected organized religion; believed he had a special connection with god; believed religion was based on man's relationship with nature.	Gibran longs for his native homeland, but also do not want to leave his adopted one.
Gilman	All female; children take precedence over everything; the society has as its major focus the nurturing of the children.	Children pursue education in what interests them; choose their own educational topics.	Rejected organized religion; believed she had a special connection with god; believed religion was based on man's relationship with nature.	The women, at least at first, do not want to leave the utopia they enjoy and return to general society.

6 Critical Analysis of *Herland*

Herland starts with three males coming into an all-female community. Each man has a different way to view women. Jeff puts women on a pedestal, while Terry is a womanizer, using women for his pleasure. Vandyck Jennings serves as the narrator. He is a sociologist and is above all interested in studying the women and their community. The novel moves forward as dialogue, through question and answer. In an effort to learn about each other and their worlds, Jennings asks Ellador questions and she responds, asking him questions in return and receiving answers. It is in this manner that Gilman conveys to the reader her impression of conditions in the world and what she thinks will make a more equitable society.

Gilman contributed to the development of feminist theory through her writing of *Herland*. Although she used a male as her main character, there were many indications of the impact of Gilman's experiences as a woman, making *Herland* an "influential work on gender as a social construct" (Cavataro 1). Gilman constructs Herland as a Utopian society, supposing that if women were given the proper significance, the focus would be on human values, not masculine ones (Kamal 396).

In *Herland* Gilman strived to show her belief that "the female is the race type, and the male, originally but a sex type" and show that when "we learn to differentiate between humanity and masculinity we shall give honor where honor is due" (Lant 293). Gilman shows the perceptions of males when she has the narrator of *Herland* say, upon his first glimpse of the country, "Why, this is a civilized country! . . There must be men" (Gilman 11).

Gilman used the three male characters to represent what she believed was men's attitude toward women. She also used them to symbolize some of her own sexual experiences (Salinas). The men, Jennings especially, find it hard to accept that the women have a technologically advanced society that functions without a man present. He studies all the institutions of their society and is open to the idea that their society is as good as his own. By the end of *Herland,* he convinces Ellador to marry him, though she has no concept of what that means. Gilman spotlights the attitude of men toward women when the three men first arrive. They are ready to fight because they cannot imagine a society run only by women, and were expecting to find men somewhere, ready to attack, as was the nature of men, Gilman believed. In *Herland,* though each of the three men fall in love with a different woman, only her idyllic Jennings refrains from a sexual relationship. However, he does marry and leave *Herland* with his bride. Jennings's perspective is well known, but also calls into question our perspective on civilization, when Gilman has us compare our civilization, with its masculine perspective, to a new civilization for which we have no present knowledge (Lant 293).

Gilman aimed to introduce a new type of fiction, but she was unsuccessful. The patriarchal concepts of marriage, sex, motherhood, love, and education undermined the shape of her novel, even though the Herlanders seemed able to deconstruct those concepts (Lant 297). In *Herland,* Gilman designed a women's utopia where women handle everything, logically and systematically, without the help of men. Only women populate Herland until the male explorers appear on the scene. Everything runs very smoothly. Quarrelling only occurs between the women in contrast to the real world where men and women quarrel with each other, often in large, opposing groups. Gilman depicts the women of *Herland* as completely satisfied with their world. Then the residents of *Herland* begin to include the company of men, whom they have not known for two thousand years. The women then begin to consider the males as potential companions, beginning with the three explorers who have happened upon their world (Rani).

Gilman's fictional world renders the sexual procreative process obsolete. The history of Herland begins when the country was devastated and left without men. Most of the men had been killed in war and lay buried under the ridge isolating them from the outside world. The remaining slaves revolted, and the women turned against the slaves. They then learned to live in Herland without men as well as to continue reproduction without them. This reproduction became the focus of their life. Gilman depicts this bonding between the women by comparing them to a sisterhood:

> "You see, they had had no wars. They had had no kings, and no priests, and no aristocracies. They were sisters, and as they grew, they grew together –not by competition, but by united action."

> (Gilman 40)

There is no instance of rape because the women are asexual. They "will" themselves to have children. Gilman reconstructs her whole world, in contrast to writers such as Kandukuri, who only reversed roles (Lant 294).

The world of women that Gilman portrays did not choose its seclusion, but had it forced upon them by men, like the narrators, from the outside world. Outsiders thus narrate the events, resulting in questionable reliability. The three explorers are not subordinates, but seem at first suspicious and are kept under constant observation, studied by the women to become good companions (Lant 294). It is made apparent by one of the characters that gender awareness is not a part of Gilman's world of women:

> Jeff continued thoughtful. "All the same, there's something funny about it," he urged. "It isn't just that we don't see any men — but we don't see any signs of them. The — the — reaction of these women is different from any that I've ever met. "There's something in what you say, Jeff," I agreed. "There is a different — atmosphere. They don't seem to notice our being men," he went on. "They treat us — well — just as they do one another. It's as if our being men was a minor incident.

> (Gilman 20)

No doubt, Gilman used this method to show how men in her current world failed to understand women in her envisioned world. This is true until the women begin to speak up and explain themselves.

These women are aware of the biological difference between themselves and the men, and they hope they can enjoy some form of 'normalcy' based on this.

Gilman had previously written about motherhood and its place in society in her non-fiction works. She continues this theme in *Herland* and deems motherhood sacred, the only way for women to enjoy fulfillment in their lives. They must populate their world and continue their race, so motherhood is vital to them. This extreme focus on motherhood seems to suggest that without men as their companions, women would make children their utmost destiny in life:

> "Here was Mother Earth, bearing fruit. All that they ate was fruit of motherhood, from seed or egg or their product. By motherhood they were born and by motherhood they lived — life was, to them, just the long cycle of motherhood."

> (Gilman 40)

Glorifying motherhood might have served Gilman's purpose to show the achievements of women, but it also has almost an opposite effect. It restricts the importance of a woman's life and restricts her achievements. The existence of fatherless children in Herland does not bring into question their legitimacy. They are children of the country, eliminating conflict and bringing peace and contentment to all.

Gilman's women have their own language. Through this, Gilman creates not only social, geographical and cultural utopias, but a linguistic one as well. This utopian language adds to their identity of a civilized race in Herland.

> "It was not hard to speak, smooth and pleasant to the ear, and so easy to read and write that I marveled at it. They had an absolutely phonetic system, the whole thing was scientific as Esperanto yet bore all the marks of an old and rich civilization."

> (Gilman 21)

Both the women in *Herland* and the visitors attempt to learn each other's language. The explorers, especially, learn the language of the local worlds (Lant 295).

Often in the narrative, Gilman reveals her ideology about "uncivilized worlds and peoples." For example, the explorers are accompanied by a "savage" who reveals to them the women's world and directs them there. A male explorer/narrator goes into the women's world, revealing a male view on the world:

> "[T]here is no doubt in my mind that these people were of Aryan stock, and were once in contact with the best civilization of the world. They were 'white,' but somewhat darker than our northern races because of their constant exposure to sun and air."
>
> (Gilman 35)

This passage reveals the importance of race to Gilman. She associates Aryan stock with the best civilizations. She describes white women as well groomed—an important factor in Gilman's world—but not always present. The women of Herland are interested in the visitors' world, and they are not put off when the men trespass on their community. In this way, Gilman is able to portray the women as proud and assured of their own achievements. While learning about the world outside, they educate the explorers about their land:

> "Have you no kind of life where it is possible?" asked Zava.
>
> "Why, yes – some low forms, of course."
>
> "How low – or how high, rather?"
>
> "Well – there are some rather high forms of insect life in which it occurs. Parthenogenesis, we call it that means virgin birth."
>
> "She could not follow him."
>
> "Birth, we know, of course; but what is virgin?"

"Terry looked uncomfortable, but Jeff met the question quite calmly. "Among mating animals, the term virgin is applied to the female who has not mated," he answered.

"Oh, I see. And does it apply to the male also? Or is there a different term for him?"

He passed this over rather hurriedly, saying that the same term would apply, but was seldom used.

"No?" she said.

"But one cannot mate without the other surely. Is not each then – virgin – before mating? And, tell me, have you any forms of life in which there is birth from a father only?"

"I know of none," he answered, and I inquired seriously. "You ask us to believe that for two thousand years there have been only women here, and only girl babies born?"

"Exactly," answered Somel, nodding gravely. "Of course we know that among other animals it is not so, that there are fathers as well as mothers; and we see that you are fathers, that you come from a people who are of both kinds. We have been waiting, you see, for you to be able to speak freely with us, and teach us about your country and the rest of the world. You know so much, you see, and we know only our own land"

(Gilman 31- 32).

Gilman portrays a difference in the knowledge of the two groups. She portrays the wisdom of the women's country, while portraying the civilized land of the explorers as being naïve. She shows how the women's culture involves speaking openly about nature and how they understand their surroundings. At the same time, she shows how the men's culture, inhibited as it is, is unable to accept and share natural existence, considering it unnatural and taboo. Although the men try to convince the women that they can not understand the "civilized" world, the reader, with Gilman's help, understands that it is the other way around – the men being unable to comprehend the female world.

Although Gilman highlights gender issues, she is unable to avoid her bias toward race and class. This brings up such issues as the sidelining of people who belong to "other" parts of society, even though she attempts to champion women. This raises questions about why utopias and dystopias sideline parts of society that have been "othered." It also gives rise to the question that if other marginalized parts of society were to write of utopia, what would it look like? Gilman's Utopian novel presents a positive vision of the capability of the feminine spirit. She changes the private world of mother/child in the individual home to a community of mothers/children in a socialized land (Lant 291).

Gilman's *Herland* was revolutionary and was accepted with trepidation by many in the literary world. Sandra Gubar says Gilman fulfilled her purpose of "decentering definitions of the real woman, the total woman, the eternal feminine." However, the shape of her novel undermines the vision of women as strong and supportive. Gubar says that the shaping of the novel negates the vision of the women in Herland as agents of their own experience. While Gilman portrays women as not to being subject to rape, masculine domination over feminine power, she loses that advantage by focusing on the issue of Terry and Alima, and their sexual union, on the potential violence involved. According to Gubar, Gilman allows patriarchal values to overcome the feminist focus of her text (142).

Since there is no sex for pleasure alone in Herland, and women are not dependent on men for their livelihood, they have equality and sharing that would otherwise be unavailable to them. According to Ann Lane, the inhabitants of Herland feel all the effects of liberation. She mentions the ideas of Herland that differ from the outside world. There is class equality, communal child rearing, no sex or violence by males, no work assignments based on gender, intense mother/child bonds, idealized homes, and maintenance of social order using persuasion and consensus (Lane).

As the women attempt to learn about the world of the visitors by asking questions, the male visitors share much about their own world. The women of Herland first learn of the use of abortion, birth control, and a harsh patriarchal God. Sometimes the differences in the two worlds seem comical, as when the women are appalled at depriving a calf of its mother's milk, and Somel asks "Has the cow no child?" (Gilman 48). However, whether the comparisons are comical or gut wrenching, as when they first learn of abortion, they serve to affect our consciousness, as well as to reshape the narrator's consciousness about naturalness, sex roles, and sexuality as understood at their time. Vandyck explains:

> I found that much, very much, of what I had honestly supposed to be a physiological necessity was a psychological necessity, or so believed. I
>
> found, after my ideas of what was essential had changed, that my feelings changed also.
>
> (Gilman 128)

There is "no sex-feeling" in Herland; society is built upon the principles of motherhood and sisterhood rather than upon artificial sex distinctions: these women, "whose essential distinction of motherhood was the dominant note of their whole culture" (58). "You see, they had no wars. They had no kings, and no priests, and no aristocracies. They were sisters and as they grew, they grew together not by competition, but by united action" (Gilman 60).

Gilman experienced difficulty in her goal of changing society's consciousness about certain issues because the consciousness she wanted to change had been formed by a set of values she did not agree with. She was addressing an audience that had values contrary to those she sought to instill in her readers (Lant 295). Problems of language and representation made Gilman's job even more difficult. She tried to create or discover a language for the concepts that she presented and her culture did not yet recognize them. How could she reshape the understanding of women and thus change their lives for the better? Though she understood the power of literature to shape her readers' consciousness, she also was aware of the extreme difficulty of using traditional form of address to shape her radical and transforming ideas (Lant 295).

Central to *Herland* are Gilman's ideas about ethics and the power of language to change perceptions. In sharing the idea of this matriarchal and utopian community, she makes language a political issue. The result is that the women's community thrives; they have no war, conflict, rape, or misery. The narrator explains that this "miracle" of the country is that the basic process of life – birth – does not require the aid of men, nor do other aspects of their life require men. This allows a maternal and non-violent life in Herland. This woman-centered culture shapes Herland's creativity as well. Gilman gives her readers a view of a more ethical, instructive, human literature than that produced in patriarchy, as would befit her visionary society (Lant 297).

Terry criticizes the literature of Herland, when the men are forced to read children's books, which Terry finds boring, calling them "pretty punk literature" (Gilman 44). Gilman uses his comment to reveal that Herland's literature was not satisfactory to Terry because it did not address his interests in life; namely, romance, adventure, and men. "Can't expect stirring romance and wild adventure without men, can you?" the narrator asks (Gilman 44).

A further problem Gilman faced in *Herland* is that her novel has male characters in order to contrast what is real and what is imaginary in her utopia. She has to compare Herland to the men's world to show the contrast she is striving to reveal. Vandyck explains his view of the differences between fiction and reality by observing, "There were no adventures because there was nothing to fight" (Gilman 49). In its art and literature, Herland does not suffer the tension and brutality of the narrator's art and literature because it does not have to suffer those tensions and brutalities of the turn-of-the-century world. Life is ideal in Herland, but its art is dull, and Vandyck agrees with Terry when he defames the drama:

"I tell you the higher grades of life are reached only through struggle, combat. There's no Drama here. Look at their plays! They make me sick."

He rather had us there. The drama of the country was to our taste rather flat. You see, they lacked the sex motive and, with it jealousy. They had no interplay of warring nations, no aristocracy and its ambitions, no wealth and poverty opposition.

(Gilman 99)

Gilman appears to have trouble separating the suffering and conflict in the real world from her literature about *Herland*. She focuses upon conflict and sexual prowess in her novel. The sexual content is the main aspect of the conflict she shows. She could have shaped the novel in such a way as to show that there can be a good novel without sexual content, adventure, or romance. Gilman fills *Herland* with aggressive, assaultive, and negative sexuality. All aspects of the novel, plotting, use of suspense and characterization, and language build on the sexual content (Lant 299). Vandyck makes obvious his feelings on the sexual challenge in the choice of words he uses: the idea of Herland is not compelling, interesting, or intriguing. It is "attractive."

In the novel, the three men are not adventurers or explorers, or after fortunes in Herland. They are characterized by their relationship with women, with their sexuality and masculinity. The virginal and undiscovered country of Herland gives the men a chance to show their virility with the Amazonian women. At the very beginning of the story, the narrator begins by focusing on the women as objects, mentioning their appearance: "Nobody will ever believe how they looked" (Gilman 1). He even refers to the land in sexual terms, saying the "strange and terrible Woman Land" is reachable only by traveling through an untamed, feminine wild zone: "a dark tangle of rivers, lakes, morasses, and dense forests" (Gilman 2). The explorers believe they will conquer Herland, either civilizing it or finding a masculine civilization there. As scientists, they intend to make sense of this unusual land.

Herland is, in ideological and metaphorical terms, feminine. It holds with matriarchal values, being a sisterhood. However, the explorers display their patriarchal powers; sometimes trying unsuccessfully to demonstrate what they believe is their superior intelligence. They continually show their masculinity. When Terry is anticipating his engagement, he speaks of the "glittering attractions" of Feminisia while "fingering that impressive mustache of his" (Gilman 7). Gilman shows how the narrator cannot avoid his masculine bias when she writes of the conflict between Herland and the visitors. He mentions that the story he wrote was from memory only and that it might have been different if he had his notes: "This is written from memory, unfortunately. If I could have brought with me the material I so carefully prepared, this would be a very different story" (Gilman 1). Gilman uses the sexual tension in the conflict between masculine and feminine ideologies when she hints at the threat behind these sexual tensions. This makes *Herland* become a love story, one in which marriage is not the ultimate goal but instead, the consummation of marriage.

Terry's intentions in his pursuit of the women of Herland are not exactly honorable. They are rather racy, and the novel develops anxiety in readers about whether or not Terry will be successful in his pursuits, and exactly how he will accomplish his goals. Gilman further plays on anxiety in the novel by stressing how the men get sexually frustrated. These men, she says, are rendered helpless by the women, whereupon they begin to feel "like a lot of neuters" (Gilman 26). There are three recognizable questions that arise when reading *Herland*. These comprise an ideological question, a personal one, and a political one. They are:

- Ideological: How does American patriarchal culture equate with Herland's matriarchal one?

- Personal: Will the men be able to convince their wives to have a sexual relationship?

- Political: Will the men overpower Herland and convince the women to adopt sexuality instead of parthenogenesis?

All three questions can be combined into one basic question. This question is will Terry ultimately force himself on Alima and rape her. Both Gilman and Terry have hinted at this from the beginning of the novel.

Terry's negative power has been there from the beginning, casting a negative feeling in novel. He may not have raped Alima, but the war and love throughout his story, the story that Gilman is telling, makes him a partner in the rape of Gilman's own text. Her handling of masculine brutality and the significance she gives it is as if she raped her own text. It is what the novel is about, a tale driven by rape as its motivation, tension, and audience interest. Gilman threatens her readers with the implied violence of Terry and the vulnerability of Alima. She compels her audience to read on to investigate and confirm what Terry will do (Lant 303).

Despite these flaws, the novel is quite plausible. It is believable, even expected, that Terry would vigorously, though not always honorably, seek a sexual relationship with Alima. He is the ideal character for it. He is a male that has been shaped by the social and psychological world of nineteenth-century America. He represents the archetypal American hero. Gilman follows the literary conventions of her time. The literary world would possibly have not allowed a novel depicting a matriarchal society with her ideology. She may have found she could not do what she envisioned, write a new story, a woman's story. Her interpretive community of one may not have been enough to convince her audience to accept these new literary standards. She thus compromised her own convictions to conform to the current set of literary conventions. We might even view Gilman as a victim of her place, time, and literary conventions. We are not necessarily constrained to view the novel as a failure on Gilman's part to portray her vision, but more likely, it is a catalog of the literary limitations of her time and experiences (Lant 305).

7 Analyzing *Herland* as Related to Four Institutions of Culture

7.1 Family

Gilman takes pains to reveal the common social practice of subduing the humanity of the female, showing in the novel *Herland* the virtues of a utopian society of women only. Thus, the women become the ruling factor, as there are no men. Family is the whole society of women and their children. The women collectively make decisions for the whole community (Kamal 398). Gilman, in having the women share their history with Van and the men, shows how important the daughters, the only children, are to the women.

> They began at once to plan and build for their children, all the strength and intelligence of the whole of them devoted to that one thing. Each girl, of course, was reared in full knowledge of her Crowning Office, and they had, even then, very high ideas of the molding powers of the mother, as well as those of education. Such high ideals as they had! Beauty, Health, Strength, Intellect, Goodness—for these they prayed and worked.
>
> (Gilman 50)

The women of *Herland* have no concept of marriage or family outside of their concept of providing and caring for children. They have the purest interpretation of love, marriage, and family in their great, universal love for each other and their nurturing of those women who would carry their children, as Van narrates:

> Two thousand years of one continuous culture with no men. Back of that, only traditions of the harem. They had no exact analogue for our word home, any more than they had for our Roman-based family. They loved one another with a practically universal affection, rising to exquisite and unbroken friendships, and broadening to a devotion to their country and people for which our word patriotism is no definition at all.

(Gilman 80).

One way that conventional expectations of women and the values of *Herland* dovetail is when that Gilman addresses the sanctity of motherhood. This is borne out when Ellador, in explaining to Van the importance of children in their society says, "The children in this country are the one center and focus of all our thoughts. Every step of our advance is always considered in its effect on them—on the race" (Gilman 57). Van attempts to share what Ellador had explained to him about how they all became one family over the years. This was exceptional since there were no males in their society. Van explains a few matrons survived and bore children, males who died. They work together for nearly ten years, growing more attached and stronger. Finally, one has a child, which is considered a miracle as no male is involved: "they decided it must be a direct gift from the gods, and placed the proud mother in the Temple of Maaia—their Goddess of Motherhood—under strict watch. And there, as years passed, this wonder-woman bore child after child, five of them—all girls" (Gilman 48). Van then proceeds to understand how this has happened, with the children involved numbering between five and six hundred, all harem-bred. Left alone in that terrific orphanhood, they had clung together, supporting one another and their little sisters, and developing unknown powers in the stress of new necessity (Gilman 49). Van explains that as the older ones died, the memory of men died with them. The women who do not bear children care for the women in the temple who bear children. This was their only means of motherhood, until one might suddenly bear a child and become one of the mothers in the temple.

This method of begetting and rearing the children, all females, results in a strong nation of women. The whole of the attitude of the women changed, Van says, from mourning and merely existing to a feeling of joy and pride. Van questions that maybe the ability to bear a child is an inherited trait by a few women. There are now one hundred and fifty-five parthenogenetic women, who are becoming a new race, Van acknowledges (Gilman 49). This shows the importance of children in *Herland*. At first, they were essential to keep their civilization in existence.

Later, they were important to improve the knowledge of society, but their numbers had to be limited.

Van narrates Ellador's explanation of how they handled potential overpopulation. He explained how they eliminated grazing animals that would take up excessive room in their small country. They then developed a "system of intensive agriculture surpassing anything I ever heard of..." (Gilman 58). He explains further that though these procedures failed to eliminate the overpopulation problem, they solved it amicably. They did not, Van explains, become predatory for more land, or struggle with each other over distribution of food supplies. He explains how they peaceably hold a council meeting. "With our best endeavors this country will support about so many people, with the standard of peace, comfort, health, beauty, and progress we demand. Very well. That is all the people we will make" (Gilman 58). Gilman appears to comment on the conditions of overpopulation and the social problems resulting from overbreeding, i.e., "of underbred people trying to get ahead of one another" (Gilman 58).

Van comments on the true meaning of motherhood as defined in the light of those mothers in *Herland*. He says that mothers have control over whether or to bear children. They are not forced to overpopulate the land and see their children suffer as a result. He explains the different belief they have of motherhood. It is not a brute and instinctive feeling. It is personal, almost a religion, involving strong feelings of sisterhood among all of the women, regardless of their area of service. He struggles to explain it, saying, "it was National, Racial, Human—oh, I don't know how to say it" (Gilman 59). He goes on to contrast his country's view of a mother with theirs.

> We are used to seeing what we call "a mother" completely wrapped up in her own pink bundle of fascinating babyhood, and taking but the faintest theoretic interest in anybody else's bundle, to say nothing of the common needs of all the bundles. But these women were working all together at the grandest of tasks—they were Making People—and they made them well

> (Gilman 59).

7.2   Education

In *Herland*, the children learn what they want. They learn naturally and continuously, though not always consciously. They learn through their senses and in their involvement in nature. They never even realize they are being taught. They are never force-fed, Van says, as the children, even babies, were in his own country. Van says:

> Their idea of education was the special training they took, when half grown up, under experts. Then the eager young minds fairly flung themselves on their chosen subjects, and acquired with an ease, a breadth, a grasp, at which I never ceased to wonder

> (Gilman 81).

Ellador tells Van that they could not learn if told what they had to learn. When explaining to Van how the expectation was for children to learn more than their mother did, and more than it was possible to teach them, Ellador said they must go beyond those before them just as their children must go beyond them in knowledge:

> Well, here is the Herland child facing life—as Ellador tried to show it to me. From the first memory, they knew Peace, Beauty, Order, Safety, Love, Wisdom, Justice, Patience, and Plenty. By "plenty" I mean that the babies grew up in an environment which met their needs, just as young fawns might grow up in dewy forest glades and brook-fed meadows.

> (Gilman 86).

Van compares the quality of the education in his country with that in Herland. He says he talked with the girls and the plainswomen from all over the country to understand their views on education. He finds that no matter which woman or girl he questions, he finds the same level of intelligence, though in different fields: "Some knew far more than others about one thing they were specialized, of course; but all of them knew more about everything —that is, about everything the country was acquainted with—than is the case with us"

> (Gilman 55).

7.3 Religion

In *Herland*, Gilman prefers the belief in a loving benevolent God to the punishing and angry one. When Terry and Van mention the practice in their country of baptizing infants and small children to protect them from damnation, Ellador gets very upset and had to go to the temple for relief.

> Her relief comes swiftly, but she is adamant that a God of love could not send children to an eternal fire (Gilman 94).

> The idea of a benevolent power that wants only good things for its subjects is further borne out by Van's discourse on their religion. Van explains his impression of their religion thus: Their religion, you see, was maternal: and their ethics, based on the full perception of evolution, showed the principle of growth and the beauty of wise culture. They had no theory of the essential opposition of good and evil; life to them was growth; their pleasure was in growing, and their duty.

> (Gilman 80)

While most consider religion to be some sense of the balance between good and evil, in Herland, there is no sense of evil. God requires only pleasure in their growth and duties.

7.4 Love of country

Gilman sets her work in a fictional, utopian place, far away from the general population. She makes note of the women of *Herland* and the fact of their agreement on all major principles of society. It had been such for more than sixty generations. They loved their country as an ideal place to grow and learn and for their children to do so as well. They had formed a society that worked in harmony and efficiency, and they were very proud of it. As Van indicates, though he does not understand it, they want it as a "cultural environment for their children" (Gilman 74).

Van, in attempting to explain the women's deep love of their country in light of his impression of patriotism as experienced in his own country, says:

They loved one another with a practically universal affection, rising to exquisite and unbroken friendships, and broadening to a devotion to their country and people for which our word PATRIOTISM is no definition at all

(Gilman 74).

Van is well aware of the reason they have such a love of their country. It is not because of any political or geographical love, per se, but because of what it means to their children and their survival.

8 Comparing the Four Institutions in Both Works

Many have written individually about *Herland* as well as *The Prophet*. However, not many have addressed information about the common traits between them. As did Gibran, Gilman wanted to help make sense of the world at the time, and make an impact. Although family was important to both Gibran and Gilman, they had quite different views on it. Gibran advocated that the love between man and woman should take precedence over that of the love for children. It was the ultimate form of family, according to Gibran. As there were no men in Gilman's *Herland*, there was not the same issue of children versus mate. The women were like sisters, whose primary goal was to nurture the children. Children took precedence over all else, as they were the future of the land.

Family was of strong interest for both writers, but the focus of family differed. In *The Prophet*, there was no direct reference to family, but marriage and children, both units of family, have very specific addresses. Gibran had strong suggestions of how the units of marriage and children should relate. For example, the couple was to nurture the children, but keep their relationship and their individuality. On marriage he says, "But let there be spaces in your togetherness" (Gibran 9). On children he says, "Your children are not your children. They are the sons and daughters of Life's longing for itself" (Gibran 10).

In *Herland*, however, Gilman portrays the "family" as being the entire society of women and children, each having a function in the unit. They believe the future of their society lies with their children: "That, of course, is the keynote of the whole distinction—their children" (Gilman 81).

In reference to education and teaching, both Gibran and Gilman appear to have similar ideas. Both advocate that in order to teach, or for a person to learn, there must be a desire on the part of the learners. Moreover, they need to be able to choose what they would learn. Further, Gibran indicates that the teacher can only impart knowledge, but cannot force learning. It appears he felt disciples must have a natural penchant for the subject.

> The astronomer may speak to you of his understanding of space, but he cannot give you his understanding.
>
> The musician may sing to you of the rhythm which is in all space, but he cannot give you the ear which arrests the rhythm nor the voice that echoes it.
>
> And he who is versed in the science of numbers can tell of the regions of weight and measure, but he cannot conduct you thither. For the vision of one man lends not its wings to another man.
>
> And even as each one of you stands alone in God's knowledge, so must each one of you be alone in his knowledge of God and in his understanding of the earth.
>
> ("Teaching")

Gilman supports the same views on education insofar as learning goes beyond what the teacher shares. The children of Herland are expected to gain the knowledge of their mothers, but to also go beyond that and add to the current store of knowledge, just as Gibran states that the teacher can only lead the student so far in their knowledge; the student is responsible for applying and adding to that knowledge. They seem to agree in the area of education more than in any of the other four institutions of culture in this comparison.

In the area of religion, both authors perceive of God as a benevolent being instead of a malevolent one. Both also perceive religion as being in communion with nature and knowledge. However, Gilman saw it as more of a collective thing, as a society, while Gibran saw it as more of an individual communion between man and nature. For example, Gibran has al-Mustafa say, "Your daily life is your temple and your religion" (Gibran 35) while Gilman has Van observe, "Their religion, you see, was maternal; and their ethics, based on the full perception of evolution, showed the principle of growth and the beauty of wise culture" (Gilman 87).

The two authors differ in their depiction of patriotism or love of country more than in any other of the four institutions. Gibran's approach to love of country leans more toward the political, to laws and crime and punishment. Gilman's view of love of country leans more toward that of citizenship and the responsibilities of the people toward each other. Both, however, have a special love of the geography of the country.

There is some overlap between the two authors in reference to love of country, though. Gibran indicates that the reason for laws and punishment is the impulse to maintain truth to one's self and to one another. Gilman shows how it is necessary to make rules relating to reproduction, limiting the number of children and designating in part which women can reproduce. Even in this, there are some similarities as well, only not as many. From Gibran:

> It is when your spirit goes wandering upon the wind,
>
> That you, alone and unguarded, commit a wrong unto others and therefore unto yourself.
>
> Oftentimes have I heard you speak of one who commits a wrong as though he were not one of you, but a stranger unto you and an intruder upon your world. ... [T]he wrong-doer cannot do wrong without the hidden will of you all.
>
> ("Crime and Punishment")

And from Gilman, through Van's observations, we see a similar view of religion, of a common responsibility.

> And how did those women meet it?
>
> Not by a "struggle for existence" which would result in an everlasting writhing mass of underbred people trying to get ahead of one another... .
>
> They sat down in council together and thought it out. Very clear, strong thinkers they were. ...

Table 5 Comparison of cultural themes

Theme	Gilman	Gibran
Women (feminism)	Women were not valued, but were considered to be only for the husband's and children's needs	Women were respected as needing protection; they were loved for their person, not their function
Love	Loved women more than men; viewed love as that shown toward children	Felt love was the basis of everything; he even felt hate was related to love because it was the opposite
Religion	Rejected organized religion; felt she had a special relationship to god; felt nature defined a person's religion	Rejected organized religion; felt he had a special relationship to god; felt nature defined a person's religion
Politics	Was very active in women's politics; did not accept political masses; struggled for rights	Got involved political through his writings; wanted to meld east and west, but keep the important parts of each
Utopia	Believed in utopia, but only without men; in some writings her utopia included men, but the women were the strongest characters	Believed in utopia; much of is writing was instruction to individuals in how to enjoy personal utopia
Family	Children were the most important in her writings; did not endorse men in her writings, or at least on a weakened level	Love for all family members were important; promoted love between and husband and wife as the most important
Education	Believed children were best educated when allowed to choose what they learned; advocated higher education for women to help them gain freedom from male oppression	Believed that teachers should not try to force their ideas on the student, that they should instead endorse the students ideas when teaching; believed a student learned best when allowed to follow their interests

Conscious Makers of People. Mother-love with them was not a brute passion, a mere "instinct," a wholly personal feeling; it was—a religion.

It included that limitless feeling of sisterhood, that wide unity in service which was so difficult for us to grasp.

(Gilman 58)

Although Gibran's and Gilman's views on religion are not identical, they are quite similar in the responsibility that is expected of all citizens. They both see God as a benevolent being, experienced in part through nature and the sense of self one enjoys.

Though they were different genders, and lived in very different societies, both had more similarities than differences. Both were strong influences on the literature of their environments.

9 Conclusion

The comparative analysis of *The Prophet* and *Herland* in this study showed how much Khalil Gibran and Charlotte Gilman were similar, though they were from very different societies, with only the timeline in common. The geographical location from which each writer presented had an impact on that writer. In the case of Gibran, he had two country loyalties. Gilman was similar in that she lived in over twenty places in the country, so she experienced this from a different viewpoint than if she had been only from one area. Gilman experienced life as a woman in a time when society did not accept women as equals to men, and Gibran experienced life as a man with the same attitude, but from the perspective of a country and society where respect for women was common and often they were responsible for helping support a displaced family in America.

There are obvious areas of common themes between *Herland* and *The Prophet* in all the four major institutions of a culture: family, religion, education, and patriotism. However, there are differences as well. Gilman wanted to change her world; Gibran wanted to help make sense of his world by understanding it. He did want to give everyone equality, as he believed that was what was "right." However, both had definite ideas about family, religion, education, and patriotism. Even though they were not identical, they were parallel.

10 Future studies

Since there are other comparative scholarly analyses of these two works, and no exact comparison of the realms of society in which they moved, even though at parallel times, it is difficult to find expert information to draw upon for analyzing these two works. A thorough examination of the two, aligning them for commonality and differences, yields the means for a comparative analysis, though it is limited in the scope of this paper. A more thorough examination of the period would be beneficial, looking at political and societal issues, and examining the two writers' responses to those political and societal issues.

Suggestions include examining other literature of the era, noting common themes among them. An examination of both fiction and nonfiction should give a more thorough understanding of the issues involved. It was suggested that Gilman would have preferred to present her ideas as a nonfiction work but felt it would not be accepted from a woman as well as would a fiction work.

Among suggestions for further study would be a look at political, historical, social, and literary ideas. Each of these have significant impacts on any writer, and would be beneficial to examine in order to get a better sense of the time, being able to take into account all aspects in doing a comparative analysis. Such aspects include the political and societal views of Mahjar literature, Arab immigration as well as immigration in general, feminism ideas of the time, and the place of women in the work force and home spheres. The Industrial Revolution was a factor of the time, as was communal home institutions. Though not examined in this paper, each of these had a significant impact.

Another factor that would be beneficial to examine is the writing style and language of the two works. This would help to compare the attitude of each writer on the circumstances of their time. There are many works written about Gibran's spiritual writing style and poetic language; however, not so much about Gilman's writing style. Both writers were well educated and delved deeply into their views of the culture of their time.

Bibliography

Acocella, Joan. "Prophet Motive: The Gibran Phenomenon." *The New Yorker* 7 January 2008. http://www.newyorker.com/ magazine/ 2008/01/07/prophet-motive. Web. Retrieved 12 July 2015.

Adegboyega, Badmus Murtada. "Migration, Literature and Cultural Identity: The Case of Arab Emigrants to the United States in the Late Nineteenth and Early Twentieth Centuries." *The Social Sciences* 5.4 (2010). http://www.medwelljournals.com/ fulltext/ ?doi=sscience.2010.355.358. Web. Retrieved 8 Feb 2015.

Al-Khazaji, Niaa hussain Fahmi, Mardziah Hayati Abdullah, and Bcc Eng Wong. "Critical Reading of Gibran's World in *The Prophet*." *English Language and Literature Studies* 3.4 (2013): 13-21. http://www.ccsenet.org/journal/index.php/ ells/article/ view/ 32254/18816. Web. Retrieved 10 Feb 2015.

Allen, Polly Wynn. *Building Domestic Liberty: Charlotte Perkins Gilman's Architectural Feminism*. Amherst: University Of Massachusetts Press, 1988. Print.

American-Arab Anti-Discrimination Committee. Lesson Plan: The Life and Work of Gibran. http://www.Adc.org/ education/ lesson-plan-the-life-and-work-of--Gibran. Web. Retrieved 8 Feb 2015

Baumgartner, Mark. "Realism: The Second American Revolution." *Common Room On-line Journal*. Ed. Lori Haslem. 2.2 (1998): 1-5. http://departments.knox.edu/engdept/common room/ Volume _ Two/ number_one/mbaumgar/print.html. Web. Retrieved 12 Sept. 2014.

Beekman, Mary. "Charlotte Perkins Gilman 1860-1935: Her Life as a Social Scientist and Feminist." Webster University. *Women's Intellectual Contributions to the Study of Mind and Society*. http://faculty.webster.edu/woolflm/gilman.html.Web. Retrieved 10 Jan. 2016.

Buck, Christopher. "Khalil Gibran." *American Writers. Supplement XX*. Ed. Jay Parini. New York: Charles Scribners and Sons, 2010. 113-129. Print.

Bushrui, Suheil, and Joe Jenkins. *Khalil Gibran, Man and Poet: A New Biography*. Oxford: Oneworld Publications. 1998. Print.

Bushrui, Suheil. "Gibran of America." *The Arab American Dialogue* 15.1 (1996). http://www.alhewar.com/Gibran.html. Web. Retrieved 8 Oct. 2014.

Cavataro, Hayley. "The Performance of Femininity in Charlotte Perkins Gilman's *Herland* and Simone de Beauvior's *Second Sex*." *Student Pulse* 3.04 (2011). http://www.studentpulse.com/a?id=507 Web. Retrieved 8 Oct. 2014.

Cole, Juan. "Gibran – Chronology of His Life." *Juan Cole's Khalil Gibran Page*. http://www-personal.umich.edu/ ~ jrcole/gibran/chrono.htm. Web. Retrieved 1/15/2016.

Darity, William A. *International Encyclopedia of the Social Sciences*. Detroit: Macmillan Reference USA, 2008. Print.

Datta, Indrani. "The 'Blue Flame': An 'Elliptical' Interaction between Khalil Gibran and Rabindranath Tagore." *Rupkatha Journal on Interdisciplinary Studies in Humanities*. 2.2. (2010). https://www.pdffiller.com/en/project/51482665.htm?form_id=82 628382. Web. Retrieved 23 June 2015.

Davis, Cynthia, and Denise Knight, eds. *Charlotte Perkins Gilman and Her Contemporaries*. Tuscaloosa: University of Alabama Press. 2004. Print.

De Simone, Deborah M. "Charlotte Perkins Gilman and the Feminization of Education." *WILLA*, 4. (13-17).1995. http://scholar.lib.vt.edu/ejournals/old-WILLA/fall95/ DeSimone.html. Web. Retrieved 1 Feb. 2015.

Dryzek, John S. *The Politics of the Earth: Environmental Discourses*. Melbourne: Oxford University Press, 1997. Print.

El-Hage, George Nicolas. *William Blake and Khalil Gibran: Poets of Prophetic Vision*. Binghamton: State University of New York at Binghamton, 1980. Print.

Emerson, Ralph Waldo. "Self-Reliance." *The Norton Anthology of American Literature*. Shorter Seventh Edition. Gen. Ed. Nina Baym. New York: W. W. Norton and Company, 2007. 532-550.

Farsi, Rohayeh. "Fabulating Through the Spiritual: Gibran's *The Prophet* and Anand's *Bliss*." *Language in India*. 13.9. (2013). http://www.languageinindia.com/sep2013/ roghayehgibrananandfinal.pdf. Web. Retrieved 3 Oct 2014.

Feiser, J. "Ethics." *The Internet Encyclopedia of Philosophy*. http://www.iep.utm.edu/ ethics. *Web*. Retrieved March 27, 2015.

Foucault, Michel. *Religion and Culture*. Ed. Jeremy R. Carrette. Manchester: Manchester University Press. 1999. Print.

Ganaie, Shabir Hussain. *Spiritual Revival and Social Rebellion in William Blake and Gibran: A Comparative Perspective*. Ph. D. Thesis. Aligarh Muslim University. 2012. http://shodhganga. inflibnet.ac.in/handle/10603/11239. Web. Retrieved 13 Sept 2014.

Gardner, B. *Up the Line to Death*. London: Methuen & Co., 1976. Print.

Gibran, Khalil. *The Prophet*. London: Oneworld Publications. 2012. Print.

Gilman, Charlotte Perkins. *Herland*. New York: Dover Publications,Inc.1998. Print.

Goodman, Russell. "Transcendentalism." *The Stanford Encyclopedia of Philosophy* (Fall 2015 Edition). Ed. Edward N. Zalta. http://plato.stanford.edu/archives/fall2015/entries/transcen den talism. Web. Retrieved 21 July 2015.

Gubar, S. "She in Herland: Feminism as Fantasy." *Coordinates: Placing Science Fiction and Fantasy*, Ed. George E. Slusser, Eric S. Robbin, and Robert Scholes. Carbondale: Southern Illinois Press, 1983. 139-149. Print.

Günday, Hüseyin, Şener Şahin and Fadime Kavak. "Literary Influences of Gibran Khalil Gibran." *International Journal of Business and Social Science* 6.3 (2015): 148-154. Print.

Hall, Stuart. "Political Belonging in a World of Multiple Identities." *Conceiving Cosmopolitanism: Theory, Context, and Practice*. Ed. Steven Vertovec and Robin Cohen. Oxford: Oxford University Press. 2002. Print.

Hawi, Khalil S. *Khalil Gibran: His Background, Character, and Works*. Beirut: Arab Institute for Research and Publishing, 1963. Print

Irwin, Robert. "I am a False Alarm." *London Review of Books* 20.17 (1998): 26-27. Print.

Islam, Baharul. "Arab-American Literary Society : A Study." *Research Link* XIII.7 (2014): 143-145. http://researchlink.co/wp-content/uploads/issues/126/18-Research-Paper.pdf. Web. Retrieved 11 Feb 2015.

Jafarov, Vilayat and Saadat Ibrahimova. "Literary Societies That Played an Important Role in the Development of Arabic." *International Journal of Humanities and Social Science* 3.14 (2013): 200-206. http://www.ijhssnet.com/journals/Vol_3_No_14_Special_Issue_July_2013/24.pdf. Web. Retrieved 17 Sept. 2014.

Kamal, Hala. "Towards a Feminist Literary Pedagogy: Aisha Taymur and Charlotte Perkins." *Proceedings of the Tenth International Symposium on Comparative Literature – The Marginalised.* Cairo: Cairo University, 2011. 389-407. Print.

Kateb, George. *Utopia and Its Enemies.* New York: Schocken Books. 1972. Print.

Kessler, Carol F. *Charlotte Perkins Gilman: Her Progress Toward Utopia with Selected Writings.* New York: Syracuse University Press, 1995. Print.

Lane, Ann J. *To Herland and Beyond: The Life and Work of Charlotte Perkins Gilman.* Charlottesville: University Press of Charlottesville, 1990. Print.

Lane, Ann J., ed., *Introduction, Herland.* New York: Pantheon. 1979: v-xxiv.

Langness, David. "The Baha'i Influence on Kahlil Gibran's The Prophet." 24 May 2014. *Bahai*

Teachings.org. http://bahaiteachings.org/bahai-influence-on-kahlil-gibrans-the-prophet. Web. Retrieved 10 Oct 2015.

Lant, Kathleen Margaret. "The Rape of the Text: Charlotte Gilman's Violation of Herland." *Tulsa Studies in Women's Literature* 9.2 (1990): 291–308. Print.

Ludescher, T. *"The oriental is ill": Khalil Gibran and the Politics of Nationalism in the New York Syrian Colony, 1908-1920.* Ann Arbor: University of Connecticut, 2010. Print.

Majaj, Lisa Sulair. "Arab-American Literature: Origins and Developments." *American Studies Journal.* 52. (2008). http://www.asjournal.org/52-2008/arab-american-literature-origins-and-developments/#. Web. Retrieved 4 Feb 2015.

Majdoubeh, Ahmad Y. "Gibran's *The Procession* in the Transcendentalist Context." *Arabica* 49.4 (2002): 477-493.

Manuel, Frank E., ed. *Utopias and Utopian Thought.* Boston: Houghton Mifflin Company, 1966. Print.

Maznevski, M. L., J. DiStefano, C. B. Gomez, N.G. Noorderhaven, and P. Wu. "Cultural Dimensions at the Individual Level of Analysis: The Cultural Orientations Framework." *International Journal of Cross Cultural Management* 2.3 (2002): 275–295. http://www.iegd.org/spanish800/adjuntos/distefano5.pdf. Web. Retrieved 4 Feb 2015.

Mbembe, Achille. "Necropolitics." *Public Culture* 15.1 (2003): 11–40. Duke University Press.. Print.

Mcharek, Sana, "Khalil Gibran and Other Arab American Prophets." *Electronic Theses, Treatises and Dissertations.* Paper 2550. 2006. Web. Retrieved 4 Feb 2015.

McNeely, Connie L. "Understanding Culture in a Changing World: A Sociological Perspective." Journal *of Criminal Justice and Popular Culture* 4.1 (1996): 2-11. http://www.albany.edu/scj/jcjpc/vol4is1/mcneely.html. Web. Retrieved 30 Mar 2015.

Nassar, Eugene Paul, and Kahlil Gibran. "Cultural Discontinuity in the Works of Kahlil Gibran." *MELUS* 7.2 (1980): 21–36. http://melus.oxfordjournals.org/content/7/2/21. Web. Retrieved 4 Feb 2015

Newton, K[en] M., ed. *Twentieth Century Literary Theory: A Reader*. Basingstoke: Macmillan Education, 1988. Print.

Nisbet, Robert A. "Social Science." *Encyclopædia Britannica. Encyclopædia Britannica Online.* Encyclopædia Britannica, 2015. http://www.britannica.com/topic/social-science. Web. Retrieved 13 Feb 2015.

O'Connor, Jennifer. "An Analysis of the Antithetical Element in the Writings of Gibran." *Gibran.* http://leb.net/gibran/other/analysis.html. 1998. Web. Retrieved 8 Feb 2015.

Rahn, Josh. "Romanticism." 2011. *The Literature Network.* http://www.online-literature.com/periods/romanticism.php. Web. Retrieved 8 Feb 2015.

"Ralph Waldo Emerson." *The Norton Anthology of American Literature; Shorter Seventh Edition.* Ed. Nina Baym. New York: W.W. Norton and Company, 2007. 489-532.

Rani, S. "Women's Worlds in the Novels of Kandukuri and Gilman." *Comparative Literature and Culture. Thematic Issue: New Work in Comparative Indian Literatures and Cultures* 14.2. (2012). http://docs.lib.purdue.edu/ clcweb/vol14/iss2/10. Web. Retrieved 26 June 2015.

Reuben, Paul P. "Chapter 6: American Naturalism – A Brief Introduction." *PAL: Perspectives in American Literature – A Research and Reference Guide.* http://www.csustan.edu/ english/reuben/pal/chap6/6intro.html. Web. Retrieved 29 June 2015.

Shahid, Irfan. "Gibran Kahlil Gibran between two millennia." *Alhewar.* 30 April 2002. http://www.alhewar.org/irfan_shahid-Kahlil_Gibran.pdf_. Web. Retrieved 8 Sept 2014.

Salinas, Haley. "A Sociological Analysis of Charlotte Perkins Gilman's *Herland* and With Her in Ourland." *Discourse of Sociological Practice* 6.2 (2004): 127.

Sheban, Joseph, ed. *Khalil Gibran: Mirrors of the Soul*. New York: Philosophical Library, 1965.

Strickland, Brad. "American Romanticism Overview." *Gainesville College*. Gainesville College Department of English. 1997. http://www.westga.edu/~mmcfar/AMERICAN% 20ROMANTI CISM% 20overview.htm. Web. Retrieved 14 Oct 2014.

Talukdar, Mizazur R. "Arabic Migration Literature of America." *The Echo,* 1.3 (2013). 20-24.

Thomas, D. and Peterson, M. *Cross Cultural Management Essential Concepts*. London: Sage. 2014. Print.

www.ingramcontent.com/pod-product-compliance
Lightning Source LLC
Chambersburg PA
CBHW070533030426
42337CB00016B/2190